The E...
School ... ...ring

Chicago, ...nois

STUDIES IN HOSEA

God's Incomparable Love

Studies in Hosea

God's Incomparable Love

K. OWEN WHITE

224.6
W Hi.

Convention Press

NASHVILLE   TENNESSEE

Library of Congress Catalog Card Number: 57-12144

Printed in the United States of America
285. AL 57 R.R.D.

TO THE MEMBERS OF THE CHURCHES

IN WHICH IT HAS BEEN

MY INESTIMABLE PRIVILEGE

TO SERVE AS PASTOR

997

About the Author

K. OWEN WHITE was born in London, England, August 29, 1902, and is a naturalized citizen of the United States. Leaving England at the age of five, he lived fourteen years in British Columbia, Canada.

Dr. White earned the B.A. degree in the University of Louisville, and the Th.B., Th.M., and Ph.D. degrees in Southern Baptist Theological Seminary, Louisville, Kentucky. While in the seminary doing graduate work, he served as a tutor in Hebrew, and as Fellow in Old Testament.

Following graduation from Southern Seminary, Dr. White has been an active leader in the denomination and has served as pastor of some of the leading churches in the Southern Baptist Convention. His pastorates include New Salem Baptist Church, Deatsville, Kentucky (1930–34); Central Baptist Church, Gainesville, Georgia (1934–36); Kirkwood Baptist Church, Atlanta, Georgia (1936–44); Metropolitan Baptist Church, Washington, D.C. (1944–50); First Baptist Church, Little Rock, Arkansas (1950–53); and First Baptist Church, Houston, Texas since 1953.

Dr. White has served Southern Baptists as a member of the Home Mission Board (eleven years), as a member of the Radio Commission, and as a member of the Sunday School Board. He has been a speaker on *The Baptist Hour* and the *Columbia Church of the Air,* and is a frequent speaker at Glorieta and Ridgecrest assemblies. In 1950 he was alternate preacher for the Southern Baptist Convention.

Other writing assignments have been Adult Sunday school lessons and Adult Training Union programs for the Baptist Sunday School Board.

Dr. and Mrs. White have two children, both married—a son, Stanley, who is also a preacher, and a daughter, Ruth.

The Sunday School Training Course

THE Sunday School Training Course prepared by the Sunday School Department of the Baptist Sunday School Board is one of the major means of promoting Sunday school work. Its influence is limited only by its use.

The six sections of the course include studies in Bible, doctrines, evangelism, Sunday school leadership and administration, teaching, age group studies, and special studies. The range of the course is broad, for the field of Sunday school work is broad and requires comprehensive and specific training. Sixteen books are required for the completion of each diploma.

The study of the training course is not to be limited to the present Sunday school workers. Most churches need twice as many workers as are now enlisted. This need can be supplied by training additional workers now. Members of the Young People's and Adult classes and older Intermediates should be led to study these books, for thereby will their service be assured. Parents will find help as they study what the Sunday school is trying to do.

Special Note to Instructor

During your teaching of this book, will you check with the Sunday school superintendent and see if an accurate record of training for the workers is kept. If not, please urge him to set up such a file with an associate superintendent of training in charge. Filing materials—cards, envelopes, or loose-leaf sheets—may be ordered at nominal cost from your nearest Baptist Book Store.

A. V. WASHBURN
Secretary, Teaching and Training
Sunday School Department
Baptist Sunday School Board

Contents

Some Projected Visual Materials

For Use in Teaching This Book

THE filmstrip *Amos and Hosea* (32 single frames, with manual) presents the messages of Amos and Hosea. It may be used in the class to introduce or conclude the study.

If desired, map slide Df 67 *The Two Kingdoms* may be used for map work in connection with the study.

Other films and filmstrips relate to present-day problems, and may be shown for extra-session, enrichment material:

CHAPTER 2 OR 4—

Forsaking All Others (Film; 14 minutes; sound)
Choose Ye This Day (Film; 14 minutes; sound)
Christian Homes (Filmstrip; 25 single frames)
Your Family (Film; 12 minutes; sound)

CHAPTER 3—

The Rich Fool (Film; 28 minutes; sound)
This My Son (Film; 30 minutes; sound)

CHAPTER 5—

Return to Faith (Film; 20 minutes; sound)

CHAPTER 6—

A Christian in Politics (Film; 30 minutes; sound)
The Christian Citizen (Filmstrip; 45 single frames)
Christian Citizenship (Film; 30 minutes; sound)

CHAPTER 9—

As for Me and My House (Film; 30 minutes; sound)
The Beginning of the Rainbow (Film; 30 minutes; sound)
The Jealous Heart (Film; 30 minutes; sound)
The Lord's Day (Filmstrip; 25 single frames)

For descriptions and prices see *Focus,* the audio-visual aid catalogue from your Baptist Book Store.

Introduction

THE BOOK OF HOSEA is not a cool, detached, sophisticated study of social and religious conditions in Israel. It is the sobbing of a broken heart. Hosea's wife had deserted him for another, but still he loved her. Under such circumstances his heart was tortured beyond description. Out of this experience he grasped with rare insight the pain in the heart of God when his people forsake and forget him.

Hosea is not an easy book to study or interpret. Constantly, it leaps from one subject to another. There are very few extended passages dealing with a particular subject. Allusions are made to geographical locations, historical events, and local conditions without any explanation. It remains for us to endeavor to fill in the gaps and rightly relate these rather obscure references to the central theme of the message.

I have thought it best in preparing this guidebook to gather together the verses which seem to emphasize a certain truth and thus to pursue that particular truth as it is revealed in the entire book. To attempt to make an intensive study, chapter by chapter or verse by verse, would be exceedingly difficult because of the lack of orderly arrangement.

In some instances I have quoted entire verses. Sometimes only the reference is given. It will be necessary for the reader to have his Bible in hand at all times. Many verses are referred to frequently, since they shed light on more than one truth or deal with more than one problem.

The language of the book is plain and frank. There is no way to tone it down. To do so is to lose the force of its message. Bear in mind that it is God's Word. Desperate circumstances call for strong measures.

Hosea's message is needed in our day when sin is glossed over and soft words are substituted for hard facts.

It has been a challenge and a personal blessing to look with Hosea deep into the heart of God and to marvel again at the greatness of God's love, "in that while we were yet sinners, Christ died for us."

I am grateful for the invitation from the leaders in the Education Division of the Sunday School Board to prepare this study guide, to the librarian of Southwestern Baptist Theological Seminary for making available their resources, and to the publishers who have granted permission to quote brief passages from the publications named.

K. OWEN WHITE

STUDIES IN HOSEA

God's Incomparable Love

CHAPTER 1

I. LOCATING HOSEA HISTORICALLY
   (Hos. 1:1; 2 Kings 14:23 to 17:23)

II. DISCOVERING THE FACTS
   (1 Kings 12:16–20; 2 Kings 17:6–8, 18; 14:25; 15:10, 13, 14, 16, 19)

III. RECOGNIZING THE EXTREME EMERGENCY
   (2 Kings 15:8–26; Hos. 4:1–9; 10:5–7)

IV. INTERPRETING THE MESSAGE
   1. Divinely Inspired (Hos. 1:1–2)
   2. Growing Out of Existing Conditions (Hos. 4:1–5; Amos 4:12)
   3. Colored by Personal Experience (Isa. 19:23–25; Amos 7:14–15; 2 Peter 1:19–21)

1

A Nation on the Way Down

"And now they sin more and more" (Hos. 13:2).

HOSEA SPOKE from a broken heart. This is always rich soil for great preaching. Much of the world's greatest preaching, literature, and music has found its origin in travail of soul and agony of heart.

Who was the man Hosea? When did he live? What were the conditions of his times? What about his personal life? What caused the heartbreak that underlies his message?

I. LOCATING HOSEA HISTORICALLY

Fortunately, these questions are answered for us in the book which bears his name. His ministry occurred "in the days of Uzziah, Jotham, Ahaz, and Hezekiah, kings of Judah, and in the days of Jeroboam the son of Joash, king of Israel" (Hos. 1:1).

This fact places him in the eighth century B.C., along with such great preachers as Isaiah, Amos, and Micah. He is recognized as a prophet of the Northern Kingdom of Israel, and his message is primarily directed to Israel. His references to geographical places in the territory of the Northern Kingdom seem to indicate a personal knowledge of them which could only be true of one who

3

lived there. He speaks of Gilead, Mizpah, Tabor, Gilgal, Bethel, and Lebanon. The whole picture presented in his book corresponds to the conditions known to prevail there at that time, and he seems to identify himself with the people in such a way as to indicate that he was one of them. His references to the Southern Kingdom of Judah are secondary.

To see Hosea's message against the background of its historical setting, it is necessary to read 2 Kings 14:23 through 17:23. A comparison with the opening verses of Isaiah, Amos, and Micah indicates that their ministry either overlapped Hosea's in part, or was very close to his in point of time. All of them, therefore, dealt with some of the same conditions and problems.

II. DISCOVERING THE FACTS

Following the death of Solomon and the division of the kingdom about 931 B.C. (1 Kings 12:16–20), the two kingdoms of Israel and Judah had existed side by side. At times they maintained a friendly, co-operative relationship and at other times their relationship was strained to the point of enmity and warfare.

Although both kingdoms fell into idolatry and corruption, the drift away from God and from the things which accompany a spiritual type of worship was much more pronounced and rapid in the Northern Kingdom of Israel.

Judgment and defeat finally befell both Israel and Judah, but it was Israel which first committed spiritual and national suicide and fell before the onslaught of

Assyria, in 722 B.C. (2 Kings 17:6–8, 18). The reading of the record of the two hundred years of the life of the Northern Kingdom is marked by an oft-recurring expression which becomes almost monotonous because of the frequency with which it appears—"and he did that which was evil in the sight of the Lord." Generally speaking, the kings of Israel were a sorry lot!

Apart from a few somewhat extended passages covering the ministry of Elijah and Elisha, the books known to us as 1 Kings and 2 Kings give us merely an outline sketch of some of the main events in the lives of the kings of Israel and Judah, with a brief summary of the character and conduct of each of them. For our knowledge of the conditions that prevailed during the eighth century B.C., we have to depend upon this very brief treatment of the times as it is supplemented by the allusions made by the prophets to various events in their preaching, and on what little may be gathered from the few monuments or tablets whose inscriptions bear upon this period.

Putting it all together, however, we have enough information to give us a reasonably good picture of the political, moral, and spiritual conditions. On many specific points we would like to have more information, but we have to be content with reading between the lines. It would be helpful to us to know more about Hosea personally. That he lived in difficult, dangerous, troublous times is plain. His own life seems to have been a tortured, unhappy experience in which domestic distress and national confusion bore a great part. Possibly, a review of a few of the names and events well known to Hosea may help us to put ourselves in his place and to grasp more clearly the picture which he saw.

Amaziah, the son of Joash, was reigning in Judah when Jeroboam II ascended the throne in Samaria as king of Israel (2 Kings 14:23). Although a good man in many respects, Amaziah had rashly entered into war with Jehoash of Israel and suffered a humiliating defeat. Later, he was killed as the result of a conspiracy against him (2 Kings 14:19). He was succeeded by his son Azariah (the Uzziah of Hos. 1:1), who reigned fifty-two years. While he had many good qualities, he did not purge the idolatry of his kingdom, and he incurred the displeasure of the Lord for a sacrilegious act and became a leper (2 Chron. 26:16–19). He was a powerful military leader and greatly strengthened the defenses of Judah.

Jeroboam II had been king of Israel for twenty-seven years when Uzziah began his long reign of fifty-two years in Judah. Two strong leaders, therefore, occupied the thrones of Israel and Judah simultaneously for a period of years.

The historian who compiled the material in 2 Kings indicates the extension of the borders of Israel under Jeroboam's leadership (2 Kings 14:25) and, incidentally, records the fulfilment of a prophecy made by the prophet Jonah (v. 25b). It is interesting to note that although Jeroboam himself was an evil man, the Lord used him to fulfil some of his promises to his covenant people (vv. 26–27).

Outward prosperity was no indication of real national security, however. Upon the death of Jeroboam, he was succeeded by his son Zachariah, who was assassinated within six months (2 Kings 15:10). Shallum, who conspired against him and killed him, occupied the throne for only one month and was, in turn, done away by Menahem (vv. 13–14). His reign began with a dastardly act of vengeance (v. 16), and in a little while he found himself in desperation offering a bribe to Tiglath-pileser of Assyria (v. 19). Israel's days of independence and power were over!

It is well to recall that much of Israel's history involved conflicts with Ammon, Moab, Syria, and Assyria (and some uncertain and shaky alliances with Egypt, who never afforded any real help).

International tensions and complications are not new. The Old Testament prophets believed and taught that God "raised up" various other nations to discipline and punish his own people for their disobedience.

The century in which Hosea lived is known as the golden age of Hebrew prophecy, for it was during this period that God gave to his people some of the greatest revelations of the Old Testament period. Hosea came on the scene when the harvest of sin was almost fully ripened. Some of the greatest preaching of all time is found in the impassioned preaching of God's messengers who pleaded with a stubborn, rebellious nation to "hear the word of the Lord."

God did not promise the prophets that their preaching would always meet with success or bear abundant fruit. He did ask them to be faithful, and indicated that no matter how dark the days he would never leave himself entirely without witness.

Elijah felt that he was the only faithful witness left (1 Kings 19:10). Isaiah was given a discouraging preview of his ministry (Isa. 6:9–12): "Then said I, Lord, how long? And he answered, Until the cities be wasted without inhabitant, and the houses without man, and the land be utterly desolate, and the Lord have removed men far away, and there be a great forsaking in the midst of the land." Jeremiah faced known opposition upon every hand (Jer. 1:18–19). Ezekiel was under no misapprehension as to the difficulties of his task (Ezek. 2:3–7).

Historically, there is no record of the reaction of Israel to the preaching of Hosea. Subsequent events indicate that it was largely ignored. In spite of heartbreaking appeals, impenitent living brought final judgment upon the nation.

III. RECOGNIZING THE EXTREME EMERGENCY

Sin is an insidious thing which infiltrates the heart and life of the individual and the nation. It is also a cumulative force which builds up to a climax, if permitted to remain.

The influence of a long line of weak, vacillating, compromising rulers had its inevitable result upon the nation as a whole. Spirituality declined, ideals were forgotten, standards were lowered, habits degenerated, character deteriorated, corruption flourished, and the stage was set for disintegration and destruction.

Israel was but one of many nations which have followed the same pattern with a similarly tragic result. In her case, however, it was especially tragic, for her particular mission was to witness for God. In recent years thoughtful students of human affairs have witnessed striking illustrations of the moral and spiritual decay which has undermined the whole structure of nations.

It was true in Israel, also! The last thirty-five or forty years in the life of the Northern Kingdom were characterized by a pitiful lack of stability of character on the part of the leaders and by a corresponding confusion and lack of purpose on the part of the people. Anarchy, conspiracy, idolatry, and complacency in the face of spiritual hypocrisy were the order of the day. Among the last six rulers, one reigned for six months (2 Kings 15:8–11), one for only one month (2 Kings 15:13–14), and another for two years (2 Kings 15:23–26)!

Political intrigue and international conspiracy were substituted for obedience and faith. Panic gripped the hearts of leaders and confusion characterized the people in the closing, hectic days of a nation which had forgotten God. However, during a good portion of the time covered by the ministry of Amos and Hosea there had been an outward prosperity which gave the people a false sense of security.

Jeroboam, frequently referred to as Jeroboam II to distinguish him from the first ruler of the Northern Kingdom (see 1 Kings 12:19–20; cf. 2 Kings 14:23–28), was a strong military leader who did much to enlarge the territory and strengthen the material position of the kingdom. He was, however, numbered among the many who "did that which was evil in the sight of the Lord" (2 Kings 14:24).

Briefly, the political conditions during Jeroboam's

reign were characterized by outward prosperity and evidences of luxury and ease. Socially, the sins attendant upon wealth and luxury abounded. Princes, priests, and people showed signs of moral decay. Family life was at a low ebb. Religiously, idolatry and apostasy had separated the people from God. With some of them a mere lip service toward the God of their fathers remained, but it was divorced from the practical affairs of life. The nation as a whole was sadly backslidden.

IV. INTERPRETING THE MESSAGE

Bible scholars are generally agreed that the message of Hosea is not easily interpreted. The book is not built upon any recognizable logical or chronological outline. It leaps from one subject to another with overtones and undertones which are not easily understood or explained.

Diamonds are not always picked up upon the surface of the ground. The richest veins of gold do not always appear as the result of a casual prospecting of a given area. A careful study of Hosea's message is most rewarding. Here will be found some of the great revelations of the Old Testament. Few of the prophets show a more intimate knowledge of the nature and character of God.

1. Divinely Inspired (1:1-2)

Although we may search in vain for a convenient or clearly developed outline, there can be no question as to the divine origin of the message of Hosea. Revelation is not so much concerned with logic as with truth. The cold logic of men may be foolishness in the sight of God.

Hosea claims divine inspiration for his message! He does not claim it as the creation of his own mind. Three brief phrases in the introduction to the message establish its divine authorship: "The word of the Lord that came unto Hosea, the son of Beeri" (1:1); "The beginning of the word of the Lord by Hosea" (1:2); "And the Lord said to Hosea" (1:2).

Difficult though it may be to understand and interpret, it is God's Word and "is profitable for doctrine, for reproof, for correction, for instruction in righteousness." The very difficulties of interpretation mark it as a revelation of unusual import and value. It deals with the "deep things of God." In the study of God's message through Hosea, we stand upon holy ground!

2. Growing Out of Existing Conditions (4:1–5)

Here we have no casual, prosaic sermon prepared by a professional preacher who knows that some utterance is expected of him and gropes around for an acceptable subject which he discusses in vague generalities phrased in pious platitudes! Here is a message which is pointed, personal, pungent. Hosea says, "The Lord hath a controversy with the inhabitants of the land" (4:1), and he proceeds to say what it is in words so plain that no one can possibly misunderstand (4:1–5).

The preaching of Hosea was not given by revelation to a man who lived the sheltered existence of a hermit shut away from human experience, but came to him through the heartbreak of a man of sensitive nature who was watching his own people recklessly traveling that way "whose end is destruction."

The urgency of the days demanded an urgent prophetic message. The condition of Israel was desperate. Amos had faced the same appalling conditions with the fire of God's retributive justice burning in his soul. He could see no hope for a people so utterly sold out to sin, and, being convinced that judgment on a national scale was imminent, he had cried, "Prepare to meet thy God, O Israel" (Amos 4:12).

To the ghastly conditions which prevailed, the tender, compassionate, poetic soul of Hosea responded in a message more poignant and personal than that of any other preacher up to that time.

3. Colored by Personal Experience

Although it is divinely inspired and came to us by revelation, the message came *through* the hearts and minds and hands of men. God's Word does not follow a fixed, unchanging, unvarying pattern of expression. It bears the imprint of human personality and of individual temperament. There is nothing artificial about it. "God spake all these words" (Ex. 20:1), but in doing so he used the personality, the experience, the background, and the several abilities of the men whom he had chosen in order to clothe the message in a form that would best meet the particular need.

Isaiah spoke with the lofty vision and impassioned oratory of a world statesman (Isa. 19:23–25). It is easy to see that he was a man accustomed to mingling with men of influence and authority (Isa. 37:21–35; 38:1–8).

Amos used the plain, blunt, forthright words of a country preacher (Amos 7:14–15) and illustrated his message profusely from nature, speaking of fig trees, olive trees, gardens, vineyards, calves, lambs, horses, summer fruit, and the like.

Each of these men brought God's message to his own day and to all time. Peter summed it up in the words, "We have also a more sure word of prophecy; whereunto ye do well that ye take heed, as unto a light that shineth in a dark place, until the day dawn, and the day star arise in your hearts; knowing this first, that no prophecy of the scripture is of any private interpretation. For the prophecy came not in old time by the will of man: *but holy men of God spake as they were moved by the Holy Ghost*" [author's italics] (2 Peter 1:19–21).

In other words, godly men who were in touch with the Lord were literally "borne along" or "carried along" by his spirit. They spoke for God and under the direct leadership of the Holy Spirit, but he caused the message to be characterized by a refreshing variety of expression as he used the dedicated personality of each man to accomplish his purpose.

This is particularly true in the case of Hosea. Possessed of a warm, affectionate nature and with the gracious ability to forgive and forget, he became an interpreter of the love and grace of God. His own tragic domestic experience enabled him to understand the deep grief in the heart of God over the faithlessness of his own beloved people. Out of bewilderment, heartache, and deep, pent-up emotion Hosea spoke. Small wonder that there seems to be no orderly arrangement and that the message clearly bears the evidence of emotional upheaval.

This brief and altogether inadequate study of the background may help in some measure to explain the reason for some of the difficulties in understanding and interpreting one of the truly great prophetic messages of the Bible.

Hosea spoke to a backslidden, worldly, impenitent people who were so blinded by compromise and sinful living that they did not recognize their own condition, and, therefore, failed to realize that judgment was inevitable and close at hand. His message graphically pictures the moral and spiritual decay of a nation which was on its way down. Outward prosperity is no evidence or guarantee of security.

To a man deeply religious and strongly patriotic, the gradual moral and spiritual disintegration of his people could only mean personal grief and growing concern. Hosea saw what was happening and knew that if the present trend continued there could be only one outcome—judgment upon a national scale.

There was, and is, however, a way out. It is the gracious forgiveness and love of God. The heart of God was torn by the thought of what must inevitably happen to his people and he pleaded for repentance and return. In this plea Hosea passionately joined.

FOR CLASS DISCUSSION

1. Read carefully the book of Amos, which reflects the conditions existing some years before the ministry of Hosea.

2. Note how greatly Jeremiah was influenced by Hosea in his early ministry (Jer. 3–4; 8:4–10; 12:13–17; 17:1–4; 18:13–17).

3. Read 2 Kings 14–15 and 2 Chronicles 26, passages which give some of the historical background of the time in which Hosea ministered. Point out what these passages reveal about moral and spiritual conditions which prevailed.

CHAPTER 2

I. A Seemingly Strange Command
   (Hos. 1:2)

II. A Normal Home Life
   (Hos. 1:3)

III. Children Significantly Named
   1. Jezreel (Hos. 1:4)
   2. Lo-ruhamah (1:6)
   3. Lo-ammi (1:9)

IV. Another Strange Command
   (Hos. 3:1)

V. A Domestic Tragedy Revealed
   (Hos. 3:3)

VI. A Redemption and Reconciliation
   (Hos. 3:2-3)

2

Hosea's Faithless Wife

"A woman beloved of her friend, yet an adulteress" (Hos. 3:1).

AN IMMEDIATE PROBLEM is faced in the second verse of the book of Hosea. Questions are instantly raised in thoughtful minds. Here is a situation unparalleled in the Old Testament. God says to his prophet, "Go, take unto thee a wife of whoredoms and children of whoredoms: for the land hath committed great whoredom, departing from the Lord" (Hos. 1:2).

I. A SEEMINGLY STRANGE COMMAND

This is where the book begins, and it is where we must begin in our interpretation of its message. There can be no bypassing of this perplexing statement. An understanding of it is essential to an understanding of the whole message.

What did God mean? What is the explanation of such a strange command? Does God countenance or encourage immoral conduct under any circumstances? Did he ask Hosea to do something which was morally wrong or indefensible? Did Hosea marry a woman of low moral standards or unworthy personal conduct?

The answer to these questions must be based upon a careful study of the entire book, upon our knowledge of the character of God as revealed elsewhere in his Word, and upon an understanding of God's purpose as set forth in Hosea's message.

At least three interpretations of the account of his marriage have been advanced. (1) Some commentators claim that the account is literal history and that Hosea was commanded to marry an actual adulteress and that he obeyed the divine command. (2) Many have considered it an allegory, claiming that no such marriage took place but that the preacher invented the parable to illustrate the conception of the love of God for sinful men. (3) The majority of the interpreters hold to the view that Hosea actually married Gomer, who was at the time of the marriage a clean woman but that she later fell into sin.[1]

The known fact of the holiness of God would rule out the first interpretation as being completely out of harmony with his nature. Furthermore, the facts would not fit the situation which Hosea is to deal with. It is unthinkable that a righteous, holy God who cannot look upon sin would command his own servant to commit an act from which we would turn away with revulsion and disgust.

Further investigation into the message of the book will reveal the fact that Hosea's marriage and home life parallel the relationship between Israel and Jehovah, but this would not be true if Hosea had married a woman who was already immoral.

If the whole account were merely an allegory, it would lose most of its weight when used as an illustration of the vital relationship between the Lord and his people. Personal experiences are much more vital than imaginary situations. If this were merely an allegory, it would seem strange that the prophet should actually name

Gomer and her father. Furthermore, had this whole account been an allegory, it is extremely doubtful if it would have contained an incidental detail such as the words in verse 8, "when she had weaned Lo-ru-ha-mah." This sounds like the recording of an actual historical event. Looking at it impartially, we conclude that it certainly seems to indicate a real experience.

All the known facts lead us to the conclusion that the third interpretation is correct. Our information on the subject of Hosea's courtship and marriage is exceedingly meager, but this is true of many historical events which relate to the lives of well-known Bible characters. We must face the fact that, in many instances, we do not by any means have the whole story. John commented that if we had a record of all the words of Jesus "even the world itself could not contain the books that should be written" (John 21:25).

When we are in doubt because of the scarcity of historical material, we must be guided by our knowledge of God's Word in general, and must proceed in the direction of sanctified common sense without unreasonable dogmatism.

II. A NORMAL HOME LIFE

Hosea has been variously described as a poet, a dreamer, an idealist, and an ardent lover. His message plainly indicates that he was a man of high moral and spiritual standards and a sensitive soul of deep and intense feeling. Surrounded by a social order which had little regard for the sacredness of marriage or home life, Hosea revealed strong personal conviction about loyalty and fidelity in a relationship which he regarded as something which should be kept inviolable and infinitely precious.

We must assume, therefore, that in common with other young people he dreamed his dreams. He fell in love with a beautiful girl. He courted her and together they made plans for their home. He felt that she shared his high standards and would be a worthy and wonderful companion. Both of them were Israelites. Behind them lay the ideals and traditions of God's people. They shared a common faith in Jehovah or *Yahweh,* as he was probably known.[2]

With so much in common, Hosea and Gomer could feel that everything pointed toward the building of a happy, successful home. The day arrived when they were united as man and wife, and it seemed that all their hopes and dreams were to be realized.

Their union was blessed with the arrival of a son, and Hosea's heart must have been filled with joy and gratitude. Up to this point there is no hint of treachery and no shadow of the tragedy which lay in store for them. The picture thus far simply reveals a young man and a young woman, both of whom were decent, both of whom were sincerely in love, who had established a normal home life together.

III. CHILDREN SIGNIFICANTLY NAMED

Old Testament names usually have a specific meaning. Children were not named just because the name chosen was attractive to the parents nor even because it was a family name. Some names reflected a certain current event. Others were intended to memorialize some act of God or answer to prayer. Hannah called her son Samuel, meaning "asked of God," because she had so earnestly prayed for a child (1 Sam. 1:20).

Isaiah named his son Maher-shalal-hash-baz, meaning "In making speed to the spoil he hasteneth the prey." In the next verse (Isa. 8:4) he explains why he did so. Dr. John R. Sampey, professor of Old Testament, in Southern Baptist Theological Seminary, used to roll this Hebrew name off his tongue with evident delight and then would add, "Guess his mother called him 'Hash' for short!"

It is quite apparent that some names were inspired of God and were definitely prophetic of the character and ministry of the one named. Jacob's change of name to Israel was most significant, for it bespoke a change of heart (Gen. 32:28).

Three children came to the home of Hosea and Gomer. Their names were significant and played a part in the unfolding drama.

1. *Jezreel* (1:4)

The first baby was a boy (Hos. 1:3). God said "Call his name Jezreel." Why Jezreel? The Lord enlarges upon it in the words that follow: "I will avenge the blood of Jezreel upon the house of Jehu" (1:4).

The town of Jezreel was located about midway between Samaria and the Sea of Galilee. Ahab made it one of his royal residences and maintained a palace there. It was the scene of violence and bloodshed on various occasions.

Upon being anointed king by one of the prophets (2 Kings 9:6), Jehu immediately set out for Jezreel to wipe out the family of Ahab. A series of bloody events followed, including the violent death of Joram, king of Israel, and Ahaziah, king of Judah (2 Kings 9:24, 27). The body of Joram was thrown into the plot of ground which Ahab had stolen from Naboth.

Next came the ignominious death of Jezebel (2 Kings 9:30–37). Almost immediately there followed the destruction of Ahab's seventy sons (2 Kings 10:1–7), the killing of some forty-two brethren of Ahaziah (vv. 12–14), and the subtle trickery which resulted in the massacre of the Baal-worshipers (vv. 18–28).

The zeal of Jehu was commendable but his heart was not right, for "Jehu took no heed to walk in the law of the Lord God of Israel with all his heart" (2 Kings 10:31).

Jezreel seems to stand as typical of retributive justice. Here sin caught up with one after another and they paid the price. Hosea named his son Jezreel in order to indicate that sin was about to catch up with Israel and they could expect judgment. Possibly, the inference is that they might look for defeat in the Valley of Jezreel (or Plain of Esdraelon), where many bloody battles had been fought. (Jeroboam II was, of course, a descendant of Jehu.)

2. *Lo-ruhamah* (1:6)

A little daughter came next to the home of Hosea and Gomer and was named Lo-ruhamah, meaning "no mercy" or "unpitied." The naming of the children denotes a deterioration of relationship between Jehovah and his people. "Jezreel" announces judgment but "Lo-ruhamah" signifies a withdrawal of love. Even the mercy and patience of God must run out when proud, stubborn, unrepentant hearts continually "do despite unto the spirit of grace."

Did Hosea already begin to suspect that all was not well in his own home? Did he feel that the sacred relationship existing between Gomer and himself was also deteriorating, that love was being outraged?

3. *Lo-ammi* (1:9)

The third child arrived. This time it was another son and he was named Lo-ammi. What a name with which to welcome a newcomer to the family! The name means "not my people," or "no kin of mine." Jehovah can no longer claim the sinning, sinful people of Israel as his. He must regard and treat them as a foreign people.

Was it now that Hosea realized that infidelity had invaded his own home, that this third child was not his? Was it at this point that he began to realize the parallel between his own heartbreaking experience and the tragic break between Jehovah and his people?

At this point there appears a break in the story. No further reference is made to Hosea's home life until a startling recital faces us in Hosea 3. What happened in the meantime? What were the intermediate happenings? How does Hosea find himself in this dilemma? How can we explain this second brief biographical interlude? Let us face it and see what it involved for Hosea, and how it was used to illustrate God's incomparable love.

IV. ANOTHER STRANGE COMMAND

"Then said the Lord unto me, Go yet, love a woman beloved of her friend, yet an adulteress, according to the love of the Lord toward the children of Israel, who look to other gods, and love flagons of wine" (Hos. 3:1).

What does this mean? Who is this adulteress? Why is Hosea commanded to love her? Is God asking him to do something which will sear his conscience? Is this account in any way connected with the "wife" of chapter 1, verse 2? If so, what is the explanation?

Here again we face the same differences of opinion which we met in understanding the former incident. Some say that Hosea was definitely commanded to love an evil woman. Some say that this is another allegory. Some insist that the "woman" of chapter 3 has no relation to the "wife" of chapter 1.

V. A DOMESTIC TRAGEDY REVEALED

When God first told Hosea to take "a wife of whoredoms," is it possible that he was merely referring to the deplorable moral condition of the whole nation and identifying her with them, even though she was personally pure at the time? Isaiah identified himself with his people in saying, "I am a man of unclean lips, and I dwell in the midst of a people of unclean lips" (Isa. 6:5), yet he was quite evidently a man of high principles and conduct. Was God implying that although clean at first, Gomer had strong inner tendencies toward adultery? What does this have to do with our present problem in chapter 3? The answer is that this is a sequel to the account in the first chapter; the "adulteress" of the third chapter is Gomer, the wife of the first chapter!

The painful details of the story are not given to us, but the bare, stark facts startle and shock us. Quite evidently, Hosea's attractive bride and lovely companion of former days had deserted him for another and had continued to drift down the pathway of moral delinquency until she had fallen into the slavery of prostitution.

How did it happen? Who can fully know the answer? How do similar tragedies occur in our day? How do girls from the "best families" with a good religious background go astray and make shipwreck of life? How do husbands and wives, once devoted, betray one another? What marks the entrance to the path that leads to the "far country" of sin?

Somewhere, only partially revealed by the brief account in the book of Hosea, lies the story of a terrible tragedy in Hosea's home. Possibly, Gomer was always shallow and superficial and hungered for thrills and worldly pleasures. She may have felt that life with one as intense and deeply religious as Hosea was dull and tedious. No doubt she was influenced by the moral standards of her friends. Virtue was lightly regarded and, unfortunately, the introduction of idolatry had brought with it unnatural and immoral relationships which were identified with idol worship.

It may well have been that Gomer began seeking an outlet for her unrest by mingling with those who drank wine in their social gatherings (3:1). Passions are quickly aroused! Sin is such a subtle, insidious thing. One step leads almost imperceptibly to another.

Did some other man seem to offer her the luxuries and pleasures her heart desired? Evidently so. She forsook her husband and children and went to live with him. He soon tired of her and she became destitute and desperate. Having taken the first wrong step, it became easier to take the next. She became promiscuous. Soon conscience ceased to disturb her. She had fallen so low that she would sell herself to anyone who would bid for her!

Gomer was not the first, nor by any means the last, who has been lured from the paths of purity and fidelity into a life which seemed to offer an answer to some deep longing within her, only to discover that it was a cruel mirage, an empty dream.

Some years ago in New York there lived a young woman, a professing Christian, married to a fine, capable, outstanding young businessman. Their marriage began with every promise of happiness and success. Possibly, she had too much leisure time, or perhaps her choice of friends was unwise. Somehow she lowered her standards, became infatuated and unfaithful, left her husband and went away with another man. Her husband tried earnestly to win her back and others pleaded with her to return, but to no avail. She turned a deaf ear to every entreaty.

In the course of time her husband reluctantly divorced her and she married her companion in sin. For a while things seemed to go well with them, then suddenly the news appeared in the papers that she and her companion had committed suicide in their hotel room. She left a note addressed to whosoever might find it:

Dear Friends: Fred and I have lived in the way of the world. We were scornful of the things the preachers said. We tossed aside the statement that "whatsoever a man soweth, that shall he also reap" and "the wages of sin is death," but we are reaping the wages now!

And what of Hosea? Of course, he could have denounced Gomer and divorced her. In bitterness of heart he might have driven her forever from his thoughts. *The key to the whole book is the intensity of his love for her.*

If his book seems at times disconnected and incoherent; if there is "a nervous hurry" [3] in his style; if it seems highly emotional; if his sentences are "thrown out in brief, glancing spearheads"; [4] if he betrays an intensity of feeling toward the very thought of marital unfaithfulness, it is because his own soul was tortured by a personal tragedy.

Hosea knew what it meant to love completely and joyfully. The early days of his married life had been anchored in complete confidence—"they two" were "one flesh." Then a thin finger of doubt cast its shadow into his heart. Doubt became certainty when his wife left him for another. At first he was numb from the shock. Gradually that initial numbness passed off and amazement, grief, anger, jealousy, and despair swept over him. Sleepless nights were followed by sunless days. His was a soul in torture because of the treachery of his beloved!

The thing that hurt most deeply was that Gomer no longer loved him. She had transferred her affection to another.

Robinson says, "His passion for Gomer was no mere explosive flash of strong emotion; rather it was a consuming fire, shut up in his bones, which no infidelity on her part could weaken, or personal suffering on his part could quench." [5]

VI. A REDEMPTION AND RECONCILIATION

Could a human love stand the test to which his had been subjected? Hosea says, "So I bought her to me for fifteen pieces of silver, and for an homer of barley, and an half homer of barley: and I said unto her, Thou shalt abide for me many days; thou shalt not play the harlot, and thou shalt not be for another man: so will I also be for thee" (3:2–3).

Life had been difficult for Hosea, but it had been difficult for his prodigal wife, too. The glitter and appeal of an unlawful relationship had worn off. Disillusionment and desertion came to her. Her partner in sin left her. Things went from bad to worse. Need drove her to sell herself, and slavery became her lot.

Wretched, stained, and disgraced as Gomer was, Hosea's heart followed her all the way, and he went to her masters and bought her back.

According to Exodus 21:32, the recognized price of a slave was thirty shekels of silver. Second Kings 7:18 speaks of the price of barley as being half a shekel per measure. Evidently, he paid half in cash and half in barley.

Sin pays off! Gomer paid the price in degradation and disgrace. To Hosea the cost of her sin was the torture of an outraged love that would not and could not die. "Whatsoever a man soweth, that shall he also reap." This timeless truth was as much in operation in Hosea's day as in our own.

Sin defiles and separates! Hosea said, "Thou shalt abide for me many days . . . and thou shalt not be for another man" (3:3). There was to be a period of probation, of waiting, of cleansing, of returning to sane, decent, normal thinking. She could not come immediately from prostitution to the full confidence and perfect relation of wifehood.

Redemption is complete, but sin leaves scars. Those who play and trifle with it are playing with fire and inevitably will suffer the consequences. It cannot be laid aside at will. To enjoy its pleasures is to know its penalties also!

Hosea 1:2–7 and 3:1–3 tell a poignant, personal story, both sweet and bitter. Here is Hosea's autobiography—his love, his marriage, his home life; his gethsemane; his continuing, compassionate love in spite of unfaithfulness on the part of his companion; and his determined purpose to win her back again. This travail of soul fitted the prophet in a peculiar way to sense the pain in the heart of God when his chosen people transferred their affection and loyalty to other gods.

Against the background of God's incomparable love for the sinning, idolatrous, adulterous people of Israel, as revealed in Hosea 2:14–23, and in the light of God's command to him to forgive and deal graciously with his erring wife, Hosea was impelled to do so. The New Testament writer says, "The love of Christ constraineth us." It was the greatness of divine love in the light of gross human sin which pointed the way to the solution of Hosea's own harassing problem as well as that of his beloved nation.

Israel's response to God's gracious appeal was negative. What was Gomer's response to Hosea's love? The Bible is silent. We can only hope that there was a genuine reconciliation.

In the end, Gomer's infidelity resulted in depths of degradation and humiliation which she had never foreseen. This added infinitely to Hosea's heartache, for it tortured him to see her thus degraded. In like manner, Israel's idolatry resulted in such horrible misconduct that God's heart was broken as he considered the depths to which his people had fallen (Hos. 4:12–14).

Hosea's prophecy, "They have sown the wind, and they shall reap the whirlwind" (8:7), was fulfilled literally in Israel's case when Assyria invaded and conquered the land and removed the people. The events surrounding the final downfall of the Northern Kingdom of Israel are pictured in 2 Kings 17:1–18. "In the ninth year of Hoshea the king of Assyria took Samaria, and carried Israel away into Assyria, and placed them in Halah and in Habor by the river of Gozan, and in the cities of the Medes."

The inspired writer of this dark chapter of history describes Israel's sin as follows: "The children of Israel had sinned against the Lord . . . and had feared other gods, and walked in the statutes of the heathen, . . .

did secretly those things that were not right . . . and they built them high places . . . and they set them up images and groves . . . and burnt incense . . . and wrought wicked things . . . for they served idols, . . . would not hear . . . hardened their necks, . . . rejected his statutes, and his covenant . . . and became vain. . . . Therefore, the Lord was very angry with Israel, and removed them out of his sight: there was none left but the tribe of Judah only."

And what of Hosea? Did he live to see the disintegration of his nation? We are not told. We know only that he kept on pleading for their return to God and that he held open to them "a door of hope."

FOR CLASS DISCUSSION

1. By way of contrast read Proverbs 31:10–31.

2. What are some of the steps that could be taken by the individual, the home, or the church to help avoid such tragedies as occurred in Hosea's domestic life?

3. What should be the attitude of husband or wife toward an adulterous companion? Is divorce the only answer?

---

[1] Kyle M. Yates, *Preaching from the Prophets*, (Nashville: Broadman Press), p. 59.

[2] Old Testament scholars of today are pretty well agreed that the name of God as revealed to Israel was "Yahweh." Students of Hebrew will realize that it is closely identified with the verb "to be." He is the self-existent, everliving God. However, the name Yahweh is unfamiliar to many people and to avoid confusion, the more familiar form "Jehovah" has been used. This agrees with the usage of the American Standard Version of the Bible, which is widely known and used.

[3] Brooke Peters Church, *The Private Lives of the Prophets*, (New York: Rinehart, 1953), p. 87.

[4] G. G. Findlay, *The Books of the Prophets*, (London, England: Chas. H. Kelly, 1950), p. 157.

[5] Robinson, *The Twelve Minor Prophets*, (Boston: Baker).

CHAPTER 3

I. DESERTING THE LORD
   (Hos. 2:2, 5; 2:13; 4:13; 5:7; 7:13; 10:2)

II. COMMITTING SPIRITUAL ADULTERY
   (Hos. 1:2; 2:2–5; 3:1; 4:12, 15; 5:4; 6:9–10; 7:4; 9:1; 11:2)

III. LOSING ALL SENSE OF VALUES
   (Hos. 4:11–12; 7:2, 11; 13:2)

IV. TRUSTING IN IDOLS
   (Hos. 2:5, 8, 13, 17; 3:1; 4:17; 8:4, 6; 10:1, 5; 11:2; 13:2; 14:3)

V. FORMING COMPROMISING ALLIANCES
   (Hos. 5:13; 7:8, 11, 16; 8:8–10; 12:1)

3

The Lord's Faithless People

"They have dealt treacherously against the Lord" (Hos. 5:7).

GOD SUFFERS when his people forsake him. As Hosea agonized over the infidelity of his wife, he found himself in a position to look deep into the heart of God. What Hosea saw both appalled and comforted him.

For the first time, perhaps, he grasped the New Testament truth that "God is love." His own experience had taught him that outraged love causes unimaginable pain. He saw that the heart of God can be deeply grieved when his love is unrequited and scorned.

I. DESERTING THE LORD

The relationship between Jehovah and the people of Israel was unique. No other nation had ever shared it. "For thou art an holy people unto the Lord thy God: the Lord thy God hath chosen thee to be a special people unto himself, above all people that are upon the face of the earth . . . because the Lord loved you" (Deut. 7:6, 8).

Evidences of God's love and providential undertaking abound. "The Lord brought you out with a mighty hand, and redeemed you out of the house of bondmen, from the hand of Pharaoh king of Egypt" (Deut. 7:8). "And

33

thou shalt remember all the way which the Lord thy God led thee these forty years in the wilderness" (Deut. 8:2). "For the Lord's portion is his people; Jacob is the lot of his inheritance. He found him in a desert land, and in the waste howling wilderness; he led him about, he instructed him, he kept him as the apple of his eye. As an eagle stirreth up her nest, fluttereth over her young, spreadeth abroad her wings, taketh them, beareth them on her wings: so the Lord alone did lead him, and there was no strange god with him" (Deut. 32:9–12). "And ye have seen all that the Lord your God hath done unto all these nations because of you; for the Lord your God is he that hath fought for you" (Josh. 23:3).

It was against the background of these passages and scores of similar statements that God now said to Hosea, "The land hath committed great whoredom, departing from the Lord" (Hos. 1:2).

Again and again the Lord accused his own redeemed people of forsaking him: "Plead with your mother, plead: for she is not my wife, neither am I her husband . . . for she said, I will go after my lovers . . ." (2:2, 5). "And she went after her lovers, *and forgat me* [author's italics] saith the Lord" (2:13). "And they have gone a whoring from under their God" (4:12). "They have dealt treacherously against the Lord" (5:7). "Woe unto them! for they have fled from me" (7:13). "Their heart is divided" (10:2).

This was the very thing which Moses, Joshua, and other leaders had feared. "Beware that thou forget not the Lord thy God . . . lest when thou hast eaten and art full . . . then thine heart be lifted up, and thou forget the Lord thy God" (Deut. 8:11–14). "Now therefore fear the Lord, and serve him in sincerity and in truth: and put away the gods which your fathers served on the other side of the flood, and in Egypt; and serve ye the Lord. . . . If ye *forsake the Lord,* [author's italics] and serve strange gods, then he will turn and do you hurt, and consume you, after that he hath done you good" (Josh. 24:14, 20).

As these leaders had feared, so it happened! Hosea lived among a generation which had departed from the Lord. The departure was no sudden decision on their part but the result of a slow, gradual, inner decay. It was like dry rot in the heart, unseen and unsuspected at first. It was like a dread disease which had spread through the whole system before being detected and diagnosed. It had affected all classes of people, including the civil and religious leaders—the prophet (4:5), priest (4:9), her rulers (4:18), the king (7:3), the princes (7:3). In actual fact, they were no longer Jehovah's people and he was no longer their God.

II. COMMITTING SPIRITUAL ADULTERY

God's Word plainly teaches that adultery is the only scriptural ground for divorce (Matt. 5:31–32). No other sin, shortcoming, or human weakness is to be considered sufficient cause for severing the marriage bond.

Why, then, is adultery considered the greatest sin against marriage? Because it is a betrayal of all that marriage stands for. Marriage is a union of two persons which sanctifies and guarantees certain intimate personal relationships which belong only to them.

Each one belongs to the other, solely and completely. It is this "belonging" which constitutes marriage. In the words of Jesus, "For this cause shall a man leave his father and mother, and cleave to his wife; and they twain shall be one flesh: so then they are no more twain, but one flesh. What therefore God hath joined together, let not man put asunder" (Mark 10:7-9).

Marriage is not merely a ceremony, but is a continuing relationship. Love and loyalty maintain that relationship upon a high plane. Sin and selfishness destroy it. To give to others the high and holy privileges which should be reserved only for the marriage partner is to take away the very meaning of the relationship. Adultery is "seeking satisfaction in unlawful relations." [1]

Immorality had reached drastic proportions in Hosea's day. Virtue and fidelity were scarce. Adultery shattered the joy and peace of his own home. Clearly he saw that unfaithfulness on the part of God's people constituted spiritual adultery. This is the theme of his message. Jeremiah and Ezekiel dealt with the same theme and used the same figures of speech to illustrate their preaching, but no prophet dealt as frankly with it as Hosea.

Two elements entered into Hosea's message: first, his own experience with a wayward wife; second, his distinctive view of the close relationship between the Lord and his people. It was impossible for Hosea to separate the two things in his thinking. His wife had proven faithless and was an adulteress. God's people were faithless toward him and were living in spiritual adultery.

Hosea uses strong words to drive home the truth. They are not pretty words, but the picture he paints is not pretty, either. There was no way he could make his point and make it effective without plainness of speech. A study of the book will reveal that Hosea uses the following words: "whoredom" (eight times), "whoredoms" (six), "lovers" (six), "harlot" (three), "adultery" (three), "a whoring" (two), "lewdness" (two), "harlots," "whores," "adulteries," "adulterers," "adulteress" (one each). It may be objected that such words are offensive to sensitive feelings. Be it also said that they may shock some people into an appreciation of "the exceeding sinfulness of sin."

Christ used plain words, too. "For out of the heart proceed evil thoughts, murders, adulteries, fornications, thefts, false witness, blasphemies: these are the things which defile a man" (Matt. 15 : 19–20). Paul was pretty plain spoken, also. Read again Romans 1:24–32.

Strong words can be used in a base, vulgar way, or upon a chaste, high level with moral dignity and strength of character. Hosea's preaching follows the latter course.

God intended Hosea's message to be hard. It was no day for a soft, soothing word of comfort. Conditions were desperate. A sin-blinded people needed to be brought to their senses. A mad self-sufficiency and self-confidence had possessed them (12:8). The prophetic word was to strike like a whiplash, burn like fire, cut like sharp steel, pierce like a sword. One of the weaknesses of some modern preaching is that it waters down the message so that there is nothing to produce conviction, nothing to demand repentance, nothing to lead to a revolutionary change in life.

The beautiful thing about Hosea's preaching was that

it was saturated with loving concern. There was no note of vaunting vengeance, but only of pathos and pleading. Having delivered hard blows, he turned again to bind up the wounds of those who would respond to his message with repentance and humility.

A worldly, compromising, idolatrous people must be brought face to face with their spiritual faithlessness. They must realize that they are fully as guilty as a wife who has left a loving, faithful husband for the arms of another man.

III. LOSING ALL SENSE OF VALUES

In his preaching Isaiah had pronounced woe upon those who had lost the sense of moral distinctions. "Woe unto them that call evil good, and good evil; that put darkness for light, and light for darkness; that put bitter for sweet, and sweet for bitter!" (Isa. 5 : 20).

Dark days have fallen upon any land when there is a leveling off of good and evil, and everything becomes a dull gray instead of clear-cut black and white! The conditions prevailing earlier, when Amos preached, had become more pronounced toward the close of Hosea's ministry. He says that sinful dissipation will "take away the heart" (Hos. 4 : 11). This is another way of saying that the power of moral appreciation is lost by those who depart from God. Immoral living destroys character. It will rob a man of good sense and sound judgment, and liquidate conscience (4 : 12).

James has expressed this same truth in the words, "But every man is tempted, when he is drawn away of his own lust, and enticed. Then when lust hath conceived, it bringeth forth sin: and sin, when it is finished, bringeth forth death" (James 1:14–15). A gradual process of disintegration goes on. Thought patterns become fixed; habits of life become so completely automatic that the will loses its power.

Hosea's picture of Israel is that of a nation which had lost its ability to evaluate, to distinguish, to choose, and to act with discernment. They were light-minded (7:2) and empty-hearted (7:11).

Although they had a wonderful religious background, they had become idolatrous (2:5; 4:17), personally immoral (4:13–14), corrupt and violent (4:1–2), unbelievably proud (5:5), politically entangled (7:8), hopelessly confused (10:13–15), "bent to backsliding" (11:7), and increasingly evil (13:2). To make it worse, they did not seem to realize what had happened to them. The opiate of sin had dulled their senses to such a degree that they were spiritually insensible.

This was the pathway that led to personal impurity and national collapse. In Hosea's judgment, Israel had followed it to the point where the only gleam of hope was the incomparable love of God (14:1, 4).

IV. TRUSTING IN IDOLS

Monotheism is belief in one God. Abraham "believed God." In every possible way he showed his monotheistic faith. Moses, in the Pentateuch (Genesis, Exodus, Leviticus, Numbers, Deuteronomy), clearly teaches that Jehovah is the Creator of all things and therefore the only living and true God. The fact that he mentions "other gods" (Deut. 4:25–28; 5:6–8; 6:14; 32:16–17) does not imply that he believed in their existence as living beings but simply that they were regarded as gods by others.

Joshua re-emphasized this same faith in Jehovah, and warned against the evils of apostasy and idolatry (Josh. 24:14–20). From the time of their entrance into the Land of Promise until Hosea's day, the people showed a strange waywardness of heart and perversity of spirit. Idolatry cropped up again and again.

Solomon introduced idolatry into the united kingdom through the influence of his pagan wives. It is specifically stated that his heart was turned away "after other gods." Among these deities which he sought are mentioned Ashtoreth (a goddess), Milcom, Chemosh, and Molech (1 Kings 11:4–8). This was probably 160 to 170 years before Hosea's day.

Elijah found idolatry in the form of Baal worship firmly entrenched in the kingdom of Ahab through the influence of Jezebel, his evil queen. He dealt with it in summary fashion and gave it at least a temporary setback (1 Kings 18:40). However, there is no real evidence of any genuine change of heart on the part of the people (1 Kings 22:5–28). False prophets still abounded and idolatry still flourished (1 Kings 22:43, 53). This was approximately 100 years before Hosea's day.

Jehu was an impulsive, explosive man of action. His purpose was to wipe out the adherents of Baal worship in Israel (2 Kings 10:26–27), but, strangely enough, he did not turn entirely from every form of idolatry (v. 29).

In the Southern Kingdom of Judah the same conditions prevailed and, to a certain extent, one kingdom was influenced by the other, for there were periods of time when they were closely allied. Hezekiah stands as one of the most godly of their rulers and his reign was marked by earnest effort to eliminate idolatrous practices (2 Kings 18:4-5). Later, Josiah took strong measures to suppress all types of idolatry (2 Kings 23:6, 8, 14, 15). The failure of all these efforts to remove the curse of idol worship indicates how greatly Israel and Judah were infected by it.

The efforts to stamp out idolatry by violence failed. Temporarily it was driven to cover and suppressed, but it was still in the hearts of the people. To legislate sin out of existence or remove it by force is impossible. Being in the heart, sin can be banished only by a change of heart.

Hosea found himself living in an atmosphere of idol worship. Everywhere he was faced by evidences of it. His book is filled with words and phrases which speak of its prevalence: ". . . lovers, that give me my bread and my water, my wool and my flax, mine oil and my drink" (2:5); "for Baal" (2:8); "I will visit upon her the days of Baalim" (2:13); "I will take away the names of Baalim" (2:17); "the children of Israel, who look to other gods" (3:1); "Ephraim is joined to idols" (4:17); "of their silver and their gold have they made them idols" (8:4); "the calf of Samaria" (8:6); "they have made goodly images" (10:1); "the calves of Beth-aven" (10:5); "they sacrificed unto Baalim" (11:2); "and have made them molten images" (13:2); "neither will we say any more to the work of our hands, Ye are our gods" (14:3). These are but a few of many references to the prevalence and disastrous results of idol worship in the preaching of Hosea.

The name Baal has its origin in the Babylonian *Belu* or *Bel*. This was a title applied to their god, Merodach. In time the title was substituted for his name. It means "lord" or "master" and is also used in the sense of "husband." It became the recognized title of the supreme deity of the Canaanites, among whom the Israelites settled when they possessed the land. There are many combinations of the name, such as Baal-gad, Baal-hermon, Baal-peor (Num. 25:3), indicating that the people recognized local Baals which were identified with their particular community.

Being identified originally with the sun-god, Baal was thought of as providing warmth, light, favorable weather conditions, fertility, and good crops. This accounts for such statements as Hosea 2:5, which shows that the idols were receiving credit among the people for the mercies of God. Jehovah actually provided for them but they ascribed such provision to their local "Baal" or lord.

To add to the confusion, there had arisen a strange amalgamation, a horrible fusion of Jehovah worship and Baal worship. Some people professed to be worshiping Jehovah through his local representative or "baal." They "feared the Lord and served their graven images."

Hosea found that idolatry was deeply rooted. It was no passing fad. "Ephraim is *joined* [author's italics] to idols" (4:17). Israel as a people were "married" to their idols. This constituted their spiritual adultery, for they belonged to Jehovah.

Religious apostasy was tied in with lax morals and

unholy practices. Only the worship of a holy God can raise the moral and spiritual standards of a people and produce holiness of character in them.

V. FORMING COMPROMISING ALLIANCES

It was God's purpose that his chosen nation should be a theocracy, that is, a people governed by the Lord himself. This plan they rejected when they asked Samuel to select a king for them. In response to Samuel's prayer the Lord said, "Hearken unto the voice of the people in all that they say unto thee: for they have not rejected thee, but *they have rejected me* [author's italics], that I should not reign over them" (1 Sam. 8:7).

During the years that followed, the kings of Israel and Judah frequently failed to put their trust in God. They tried political diplomacy, military alliances, and economic agreements. They played one nation against another and followed the policy of expediency. Their political "skulduggery" frequently put them in deep water. Some of their schemes backfired. Time after time the prophets scolded the leaders for their lack of faith or pleaded with them to break off their entangling alliances.

The chaotic, directionless days in the latter part of Hosea's ministry found the leaders desperately seeking some way out of their dilemma and danger. Hosea's preaching reflects his disgust with them for turning to other nations for help. He says, "When Ephraim saw his sickness, and Judah saw his wound, then went Ephraim to the Assyrian, and sent to king Jareb: yet could he not heal you, nor cure you of your wound" (Hos. 5:13).

It has been conjectured that Jareb might be the great king, Tiglath-pileser (Pul). Menahem sent him tribute about 738 B.C. (2 Kings 15:19-20).

Another reference to compromising alliances is noted in Hosea 7:8: "Ephraim, he hath mixed himself among the people." As though to emphasize the breathless, frantic rushing from one possible source of assistance to another, Hosea says, "Ephraim also is like a silly dove without heart: they call to Egypt, they go to Assyria" (7:11). Because of their disregard for the Lord and their hypocrisy and deceit God says, "Their princes shall fall by the sword for the rage of their tongue: this shall be their derision in the land of Egypt" (7:16).

The uselessness of forming such alliances is clearly indicated in Hosea 8:8-10: "Israel is swallowed up: now shall they be among the Gentiles as a vessel wherein is no pleasure. For they are gone up to Assyria, a wild ass alone by himself: Ephraim hath hired lovers. Yea, though they have hired among the nations, now will I gather them, and they shall sorrow a little for the burden of the king of princes."

Their sin was going to scatter them to the very countries to which they had appealed for help. "They shall not dwell in the Lord's land; but Ephraim shall return to Egypt, and they shall eat unclean things in Assyria" (9:3).

Hosea returns to the same theme in 12:1. "Ephraim feedeth on wind, and followeth after the east wind: he daily increaseth lies and desolation; and they do make a covenant with the Assyrians, and oil is carried into Egypt."

The policy of expediency is not new. It did not begin with Chamberlain and Czechoslovakia, nor with the unhappy days when our nation supplied oil and scrap iron to Japan for an unprovoked war on China, nor even with the secret agreements of the Yalta Conference, which have led us into endless problems.

Individuals, as well as nations, face the constant temptation to solve problems in the realm of expediency, rather than in the realm of conviction and conscience. For Israel the outcome was tragic. "Thus saith the Lord; Cursed be the man that trusteth in man, and maketh flesh his arm, and whose heart departeth from the Lord" (Jer. 17:5). To the unbelieving human heart, human friends and allies, horses and men, armies and navies, planes and tanks, atom and hydrogen bombs seem more concrete and substantial than the promises of God!

FOR CLASS DISCUSSION

1. Suggest some of the modern pitfalls which ensnare the Lord's people.

2. Think about some of the national dangers which confront us. Are there present trends which indicate danger ahead?

---

[1] G. Campbell Morgan, *Voices of the Twelve Hebrew Prophets*, (Westwood, N. J.: Revell, 1938), p. 46.

CHAPTER 4

I. ISRAEL, THE WIFE OF THE LORD
   (Isa. 54:5–6; Jer. 3:20; Ezek. 16:32; Hos. 2:14–16; 2:19–20)

II. THE SIGNIFICANCE OF MARRIAGE
   (Gen. 2:18–24; Heb. 13:4; Eph. 5:31; Matt. 19:4–8)

III. CAUSES OF UNFAITHFULNESS
   1. Material Greed (Hos. 2:5)
   2. Rejection of the Truth (4:6)
   3. Unworthy Leadership (4:8–9; 5:1, 10; 7:3; 8:4)
   4. Compromise and Integration with Idolatrous Neighbors (5:13; 7:8; 8:8–9)
   5. Pride and Self-Sufficiency (5:5; 7:10; 12:8)
   6. Superficiality (6:4; 7:11; 8:12; 10:1; 12:1)
   7. Love of Sin (4:18; 9:1, 10; 11:2; 13:2)
   8. Disregard of the Covenant (Jer. 7:13, 25; Ezek. 16:8; 23:36–39)

IV. THE RESULTS OF UNFAITHFULNESS
   1. Disowning by the Lord (Hos. 1:9)
   2. Corruption (4:1–2)
   3. Disintegration of Character (4:6–10)
   4. Confusion (5:13)
   5. Desperation (7:11)
   6. Penalty (8:7; 9:16; 10:13; 13:1–2, 9)

46

4

The Tie That Binds

"I will betroth thee unto me" (Hos. 2:19).

THE closest of all human relationships is that which exists between husband and wife. Based upon mutual love and understanding, there is a blending and welding of the two into one.

In searching for an adequate figure by which to describe his relationship to his own people, the Lord chose the sacred bonds of marriage. This wonderful picture of the intimate relationship between Jehovah and his people seems to be suggested in Exodus 34:14–16. "For thou shalt worship no other god: for the Lord, whose name is Jealous, is a jealous God."

The jealousy here spoken of represents complete and unchallenged possession upon the basis of a mutual covenant or agreement. (Lev. 17:7; 20:5–6). Here the expression "a whoring" indicates that a sacred, personal relationship is broken when God's people turn to other gods. Numbers 14:33 uses the same strong language, while Deuteronomy 32:16–21 enlarges upon the same theme. These and other related passages contain a foregleam of the truth later plainly revealed by Isaiah, Hosea, and Jeremiah: that God regarded his people Israel as his wife, his "beloved."

The sacred relationship between Jehovah and his people is clearly taught in Isaiah 54:5–6: "For thy Maker is thine husband; the Lord of hosts is his name; and thy Redeemer the Holy One of Israel; The God of the whole earth shall he be called. For the Lord hath called thee as a woman forsaken and grieved in spirit, and a wife of youth, when thou wast refused, saith thy God."

Jeremiah uses the same figure, "Surely as a wife treacherously departeth from her husband, so have ye dealt treacherously with me, O house of Israel, saith the Lord" (Jer. 3:20). In Jeremiah 31:32 God says, ". . . although I was an husband unto them."

Through Ezekiel the Lord charged his people with desertion and infidelity in the words, "As a wife that committeth adultery, which taketh strangers instead of her husband!" (Ezek. 16:32).

The Bible clearly teaches, then, that the tie which binds the people of God to him is as sacred and intimate as the marriage bond. Hosea believed this. It is the basic truth upon which his message rests.

I. ISRAEL, THE WIFE OF THE LORD

This thought is startling, yet it ought not to seem too strange to New Testament Christians, who are familiar with the truth that the church is the bride of Christ (Eph. 5:23–25, 32; Rev. 22:17). From among the nations of the earth, God chose Israel to be his own peculiar possession. His choice was not founded upon her worthiness but upon his love. As her husband he provided sustenance, protection, and affection.

God was faithful to Israel. Joshua testified to them "that not one thing hath failed of all the good things which the Lord your God spake concerning you" (Josh. 23:14). In response to his faithfulness, God expected Israel to be faithful to him. There can be no firm and enduring marriage without faithfulness on both sides. God had entered into this covenant relationship with his people, not for a few days, not for a century, but "for ever" (Gen. 17:7).

Their sin had broken the relationship, but even as Hosea sought out his sinning wife, God said that he would seek to win back his people (Hos. 2:14–16). "In that day" they are to call him "my husband," not "my Baal." His longing to renew the broken relationship is seen in the words, "And I will betroth thee unto me for ever; yea, I will betroth thee unto me in righteousness, and in judgment, and in lovingkindness, and in mercies. I will even betroth thee unto me in *faithfulness* [author's italics]: and thou shalt know the Lord" (2:19–20). Nine times in the book of Hosea God refers to the people of Israel as "my people." A note of possessive affection characterizes his attitude toward them.

II. The Significance of Marriage

Without the institution of marriage, civilization as we know it could not exist, and an orderly and honorable society would be impossible. It is basic to a decent and stable way of life.

Human history begins with husband and wife (Gen. 2:18–24). From the very first it was God's plan that this relationship should be unique and permanent (Matt. 19:4–8). Note particularly verse 8, concerning divorce: ". . . but from the beginning it was not so." A true marriage cannot exist where either husband or wife belongs to someone else.

Marriage is a divinely planned relationship. It is the first institution (Gen. 2:24).

Marriage is a pure relationship. Man and woman were made one for the other. Absolute loyalty sanctifies their relationship. Impurity comes only in the intrusion of a third party.

Marriage is a personal relationship. It constitutes the most personal of all the relationships of life. It involves just two people who agree to become one in sharing every area of their lives.

Marriage is a permanent relationship. Sin, and sin alone, breaks it and destroys its permanence. In God's original purpose only death was to sever its ties.

III. Causes of Unfaithfulness

Why did the people of Israel forsake God? This is one of the vexing problems of the Old Testament. The writer of Hebrews says that at the time of their defeat at Kadesh-barnea, "they could not enter in because of unbelief" (Heb. 3:19).

In the final analysis, unbelief is the basic reason for every departure from the will of God. Unbelief reveals itself in failure to act upon the known will of God. An unbelieving heart is prone to be stubborn, perverse, proud, disobedient, and wayward.

Look into the book of Hosea again and inquire why the people had been so unbelievably treacherous and weak.

1. *Material Greed* (2:5)

"For she said, I will go after my lovers, that give me my bread and my water, my wool and my flax, mine oil and my drink." It was commonly believed that the local Baals increased and multiplied the crops. Whoever promises to provide food, clothing, and money is assured of a large following! Communism in our day has won millions of converts by promising a better distribution of material things.

2. *Rejection of the Truth* (4:6)

"Because thou hast rejected knowledge, I will also reject thee." Years later Paul said of men that "even as they did not like to retain God in their knowledge, God gave them over to a reprobate [outcast] mind" (Rom. 1:28). To hear the truth, to be familiar with it, and then to ignore and set it aside is always a dangerous business! Wilful hardening of the heart invites God's judgment.

3. *Unworthy Leadership* (4:8–9; 5:1, 10; 7:3; 8:4)

Many passages contain a reflection of the unworthiness of the leaders. (See, for example, 4:8–9; 5:1, 10; 7:3; 8:4). Great is the responsibility of leadership, whether it be in the home, the church, or the nation! Mark the tragic outcome of atheistic leadership in Nazi Germany and Communist Russia.

4. *Compromise and Integration with Idolatrous Neighbors* (4:15; 7:8; 8:8–9)

It has been pointed out previously that idolatry "infiltrated" the nation gradually. Some of the Canaanites remained in the land and contributed to this infiltration. Some of Solomon's wives brought their idols with them. Jezebel was an evil influence. "Ephraim, he hath mixed himself among the people" (7:8).

5. *Pride and Self-Sufficiency* (5:5; 7:10; 12:8)

At least twice Hosea refers specifically to the pride of Israel (5:5; 7:10). On another occasion he speaks of Israel's insufferable self-righteousness and complacency, even in the face of her corruption (12:8). "And Ephraim said, Yet I am become rich, I have found me out substance: in all my labours they shall find none iniquity in me that were sin."

6. *Superficiality* (6:4; 7:11; 8:12; 10:1; 12:1)

The shallow emptiness and complete lack of stability which characterized his people deeply grieved Hosea. He speaks of it frequently (6:4; 7:11; 8:12; 10:1; 12:1).

7. *Love of Sin* (4:18; 9:1, 10; 11:2; 13:2)

It is the love of sin, the enjoyment of sin, the pleasures of sin which lure people away from love and loyalty to God. Hosea says of the leaders, "They love shame more than their glory." He says, "They make the king glad with their wickedness" (7:3). He refers to various things which have attracted them and led them astray (2:13; 8:11; 9:1; 11:7; 12:7).

8. *Disregard of the Covenant* (Jer. 7:13, 25; Ezek. 16:8; 23:36–39)

A combination of these and other causes led Israel further and further away from her God. From the first she had been unstable and undependable. She was particularly susceptible to idolatry. From time to time God sent to her great leaders and prophets to remind her of her covenant relationship (Jer. 7:13, 25; Ezek. 16:8). "Yea, I sware unto thee, and entered into a covenant with thee, saith the Lord God, and thou becamest mine." Incidentally, this covenant is mentioned scores of times in the Old Testament.

All of this will indicate how fitting was the figure of the marriage relationship to describe God's relationship to his chosen people, Israel. There was to be no other object of affection; no other "god" was to be worshiped and followed. To his idolatrous people God said, "And I will judge thee, as women that break wedlock" (Ezek. 16:38). Ezekiel pictures the spiritual adultery of Israel and Judah in the parable of the two sisters, Aholah and Aholibah (Ezek. 23:36–39).

Through Moses, God had said to his people, "I am the Lord thy God, which have brought thee out of the land of Egypt, out of the house of bondage. Thou shalt have no other gods before me. Thou shalt not make unto thee any graven image, or any likeness of any thing that is in heaven above, or that is in the earth beneath, or that is in the water under the earth: Thou shalt not bow down thyself to them, nor serve them: for I the Lord thy God am a jealous God" (Ex. 20:2–5).

The husband who loves his wife will be jealous of her, and God is jealous of his people in the sense that he cannot share them with other objects of worship.

IV. THE RESULT OF UNFAITHFULNESS

The sin of adultery hurts everyone involved. It hurts the faithful partner. It hurts the unfaithful partner. It hurts the third party, who knows that he is stealing.

Hosea's heart was crushed by the treachery of his wife. Her own heart must have felt the sting of shame, disloyalty, and guilt. Forgiveness may come later on, but the facts still remain and there is no going back and removing them. Scars are left forever.

Although the book of Hosea may lack orderly arrangement, it never departs from its main theme: the unfaithfulness of Israel to Jehovah. "To Hosea the greatest of all sins was unfaithfulness to Jehovah." [1] The reason why Gomer had left Hosea was plain; she no longer loved him. Like the church in Ephesus, she had "left her first love." Therefore, the reason why Jehovah's people had deserted him was that they no longer cared!

The first result of Israel's infidelity was grief in the heart of God. To be sure, he was righteously indignant, but he was also deeply hurt. This is plain from such statements as this, "How shall I give thee up, Ephraim? how shall I deliver thee, Israel? . . . mine heart is turned within me, my repentings are kindled together" (11:8).

The second result was a complete separation and loss of fellowship. Of Israel, God was forced to say, "She is not my wife, neither am I her husband" (2:2). Sin had brought separation, for "they shall go with their flocks and with their herds to seek the Lord; but they shall not find him; he hath *withdrawn himself from them*" [author's italics] (5:6).

So far as Israel herself was concerned, the results of infidelity are too numerous to mention. They include: disowning by the Lord (1:9), corruption (4:1–2), disintegration of character (4:6–10), confusion (5:13), desperation (7:11); and the penalties that accompany such sin (2:7; 4:10; 5:12; 7:2, 9; 8:7; 9:16; 10:13; 13:1–2, 9). Let us go back for a moment to the results of Israel's infidelity and consider them a little more in detail.

1. *Disowning by the Lord* (1:9)

Through the years it had been Israel's boast that she belonged to Jehovah and enjoyed his special favor. This sense of belonging, unfortunately, did not carry with it an accompanying sense of responsibility on their part.

Amos had flayed them for this complacency and lack of understanding when he said: "Woe unto you that desire the day of the Lord! to what end is it for you? the day of the Lord is darkness, and not light" (Amos 5:18). "All the sinners of my people shall die by the sword, which say, The evil shall not overtake nor prevent us" (Amos 9:10).

In spite of a wonderful covenant relationship and years of gracious blessings, God's people had treacherously forsaken him. He now had to say to them, "Ye are not my people, and I will not be your God."

2. *Corruption* (4:1-2)

Truth which makes men free and mercy which keeps them from abusing their freedom had departed from Israel. An understanding of the nature and moral requirement of God was sadly lacking.

Jesus said that to love God and to love one's neighbor as one's self represents the fulfilling of the law. The people of Israel did neither. Naturally, therefore, they broke all the commandments. They were characterized by the grossest, ugliest sins of flesh and spirit.

3. *Disintegration of Character* (4:6-10)

It is terrible to see a nation on the way down. Hosea watched with increasing sorrow as the process of disintegration proceeded before his eyes. He attributed it to a lack of a personal experience with God. "My people are destroyed for lack of knowledge"—heart knowledge.

Power and glory had only contributed to their pride, self-sufficiency, and indifference to God (v. 7). Spiritual leadership had failed, and those who ought to have reproved the people for their sin encouraged them in it. "And there shall be, like people, like priest" (v. 9). It is suggested that the word priest in verse 4 really means "priestling." The nation was falling apart because the priests had led them astray.

4. *Confusion* (5:13)

As danger began to threaten and the nation began to realize its condition, panic set in. They turned to Assyria for aid, yet found no relief or security. The urgency of their need, however, did not bring them back to God. Modern nations are seeking relief in strange and inconsistent pacts and alliances.

5. *Desperation* (7:11)

The situation deteriorated as time went on. Hosea pictures Israel as a "silly dove" fluttering in frenzy between Assyria on one hand and Egypt on the other. Once the nation was committed to a policy of seeking aid, it was difficult to change. Complications multiplied daily.

6. *Penalty* (8:7; 9:16; 10:13; 13:1-2, 9)

The ways of sin ended in saddening disillusionment, and the way back was not easy (2:7). The sense of satisfaction departed and normal fruitfulness was cut off "because they have left off to take heed to the Lord" (4:10). He who once protected and sustained them will cause them to be moth-eaten and weakened by internal dry rot (5:12).

"Their own doings have beset them about" (7:2). Again the truth emerges that sin is its own penalty. Judgment is self-inflicted. Israel is described as a man whose strength has been sapped and who is growing old but does not know it! (7:9). In common with many others, Israel failed to realize that the harvest is much greater than the planting. The sowing may seem as a gentle breeze; the day of reaping will be as a tornado (8:7).

God draws the picture of a diminishing nation which shall be further reduced by the deaths suffered in war (9:16). Finally, he shows that idolatry had destroyed the very heart of the nation for "when he offended in Baal, he died. And now they sin more and more" (13:1-2). Increasing sin was the inevitable result of spiritual adultery. Hosea's wife went from bad to worse until enslaved. Israel had gone from bad to worse until God must say, "O Israel, thou hast destroyed thyself" (13:9).

A sacred covenant bound Israel to her God. With inexcusable disloyalty and base ingratitude, she broke this sacred tie. A wayward wife wandered away from a devoted husband.

"It pays to serve Jesus," but it costs to forsake the Lord! Spiritual adultery can only result in spiritual desolation and the scourging fires of discipline.

FOR CLASS DISCUSSION

1. Examine some of the illustrations given in the Bible of departure from God's original plan of monogamy and the resultant jealousy and confusion. For example: Abraham (Gen. 16:4-6); Jacob (Gen. 29-32); David (1 Sam. 11-21).

2. Consider the meaning of the New Testament teaching concerning the church as the bride of Christ. What obligations does this relationship place upon the individual believer?

3. Would a clearer understanding of the sacred relationship between God and his people strengthen marriage ties and deepen conviction concerning the permanence of marriage?

4. Does your study of this chapter seem to you to suggest the thought that, in a Christian marriage, the relationship between man and wife is meant to be a demonstration to the world of the mutual love between Christ and his church? Does not this concept give added motivation for using every

available channel of church organization in seeking a more effective ministry to the homes in your church community. Can you suggest some ways in which such a ministry on the part of your church could be strengthened?

---

[1] Rollin H. Walker, *Men Unafraid* (out of print).

CHAPTER 5

I. **The Danger of Forgetfulness**
   (Psalm 103:2; Hos. 4:6; 8:14)

II. **The Road to Backsliding**
   1. Lack of Knowledge (Hos. 4:6)
   2. Pride (5:5; 7:10)
   3. Instability (6:4)
   4. Worldliness (7:8)
   5. Corruption (9:9)
   6. Idolatry (13:2)

III. **Centers of Idolatry**
   1. Gilgal (Hos. 4:15; 9:15; 12:11)
   2. Beth-aven (4:15)
   3. Mizpah (5:1)
   4. Tabor (5:1)
   5. Gibeah (9:9)
   6. Ramah (5:8)
   7. Gilead (6:8)
   8. Samaria (7:1; 8:5, 6; 10:5, 7; 13:16)
   9. Baal-peor (9:10)

IV. **Growing a Habit**
   (Hos. 7:2, 9; 9:7; 8:7; 13:3)

5

Bent to Backsliding

"For Israel slideth back as a backsliding heifer" (Hos. 4:16).

LOSING GROUND, losing time, losing strength, losing opportunity, losing influence—this is backsliding! Faith falters, vision grows dim, love cools off, fellowship is broken, and the Holy Spirit is grieved. What is more common among modern believers than backsliding? The word covers a multitude of sins, but the end result is always broken fellowship and spiritual decline.

Perhaps, occasional periods of cooling off and losing the keen sense of personal obligation may be expected, but habitual and constant backsliding is another matter. Through Hosea, the Lord charged his people with a perverse and stubborn inclination to have their own way, which had resulted in just such backsliding.

I. THE DANGER OF FORGETFULNESS

"Bless the Lord, O my soul, and forget not all his benefits" (Psalm 103:2). Forgetfulness and ingratitude usually walk hand in hand. In his poem "Recessional" Rudyard Kipling called upon his nation—and ours—to remember our primary need for dependence upon God. The prophets of the Old Testament called upon the people ever to keep some things in remembrance.

Israel was doomed but did not know it. She was delinquent and dirty but did not care. Her condition is contained and explained in the words, "Thou hast forgotten the law of thy God" (4:6).

"The law" is not to be thought of as merely the basic Ten Commandments. To those great principles which govern the relationship of man to God and to his fellow-man, God had added much more. He had explained and interpreted his law in the light of human personality and human rights and privileges so that he could say to his people, "I desired mercy, and not sacrifice; and the knowledge of God more than burnt offerings" (6:6).

Fellowship with God is always closely associated with the right sort of relationship with others. "Pure religion and undefiled before God and the Father is this, To visit the fatherless and widows in their affliction, and to keep himself unspotted from the world." "If ye fulfil the royal law according to the scripture, Thou shalt love thy neighbour as thyself, ye do well" (James 1:27; 2:8).

"If a man say, I love God, and hateth his brother, he is a liar: for he that loveth not his brother whom he hath seen, how can he love God whom he hath not seen?" (1 John 4:20).

"Render therefore to all their dues: tribute to whom tribute is due; custom to whom custom; fear to whom fear; honour to whom honour. Owe no man any thing, but to love one another: for he that loveth another hath fulfilled the law" (Rom. 13:7-8).

To forget the great underlying truths upon which godly living is based will result in broken fellowship.

Hosea's generation had forgotten. No wonder they were a backslidden people. Their conduct in human relations clearly showed that God's law was no longer their guide (Hos. 4:1–2, 8; 6:8–9; 7:1; 12:7).

God's law is not a harsh, hard, impersonal, external code. It is an inner thing. It may be written upon tables of stone at times, but fundamentally it is written in the heart. Paul, in speaking of the Gentiles, says that they "do by nature the things contained in the law . . . which shew the work of the law written in their hearts" (Rom. 2:14–15). Isaiah says, "Hearken unto me, ye that know righteousness, the people in whose heart is my law" (Isa. 51:7). Jeremiah speaks of a new covenant in these words, "But this shall be the covenant that I will make with the house of Israel; After those days, saith the Lord, I will put my law in their inward parts, and write it in their hearts; and will be their God, and they shall be my people" (Jer. 31:33).

"For Israel hath forgotten his Maker" (Hosea 8:14). Neglect, carelessness, lack of loyalty, material interests, lightmindedness—these are the things which pave the way to forgetfulness. It must have seemed to Hosea that memory of God's faithfulness no longer played a part in the life of Israel.

II. THE ROAD TO BACKSLIDING

In his book *The Twelve Minor Prophets* Robinson has noted seven steps in the downfall of Israel as recorded by Hosea:[1] (1) lack of knowledge (4:6); (2) pride (5:5); (3) instability (6:4); (4) worldliness (7:8); (5) corruption (9:9); (6) backsliding (11:7); (7) idolatry (13:2).

Should these symptoms be regarded as cause or effect? Did Israel's backslidden condition lead to these things, or were they the steps which resulted in her backslidden condition? Looking into the record, conviction grows upon us that these were the steps which led downward from the high levels of fellowship with God to the dreary plains of "Backsliders' Land."

Recall that the names of Hosea's children indicated a gradual deterioration of relationship between the Lord and his people. It is a picture of drifting further and further from God. "And now they sin more and more" (13:2). Look briefly at the downward steps which have been suggested:

1. *Lack of Knowledge* (4:6)

This lack does not imply that the people have been left in ignorance of the truth and need to be informed, but that they have deliberately refused to accept and follow the truth. God says, "Thou hast *rejected* [author's italics] knowledge" (4:6). By the knowledge of God, Hosea means a personal experience with God. He is not thinking of an intellectual grasp of the facts but of a heart knowledge which bears fruit. He returns to this theme frequently. Hosea 2:20 can mean nothing less than a warm, vital, personal experience with God: "I will even betroth thee unto me in faithfulness: and thou shalt know the Lord." There is to be a growing understanding expressing itself in personal relationships.

"Then shall we know, if we follow on to know the Lord" (6:3). This had been Israel's weakness! They did not follow on. There was a sad lack of stability, of determination to maintain consistent fellowship with God. Such lack of personal experience and consistent fellowship will always result in drifting.

Hosea implied that when the emergency arrived the nation would profess to know God. "Israel shall cry unto me, My God, we know thee" (8:2). However, the entire context indicates that it was a false, shallow, spurious profession.

2. *Pride* (5:5; 7:10)

Faith in God involves reliance and dependence upon him. In spite of the confusion and chaos which had befallen them, the people of Israel were too self-sufficient to seek God. "And the pride of Israel testifieth to his face: and they do not return to the Lord their God, nor seek him for all this" (7:10).

Israel as a nation had surrendered to compromise, and could best be described as "a cake not turned" (7:8). Her strength was wasting away, and signs of premature old age were in evidence, yet her very pride and self-sufficiency blinded her to her own condition. A sickening self-satisfaction characterized her.

3. *Instability* (6:4)

"O Ephraim, what shall I do unto thee? O Judah, what shall I do unto thee? for your goodness is as a morning cloud, and as the early dew it goeth away."

What illustrations could surpass these? The people were as elusive and unstable as quicksilver. Whatever tokens of righteous living they showed were no longer-lasting than the dew which dries up and disappears in a matter of minutes.

Their frantic efforts to find help and support somewhere were evidence of a fundamental weakness of character (7:11; 13:3). "Their heart is divided" (10:2). James says, "A double minded man is unstable in all his ways" (James 1:8). In faith and practice the Israel of Hosea's day exhibited extreme instability. The attempt to combine Jehovah worship with Baal worship was about as successful as combining iron and clay. Jesus said, "Ye cannot serve God and mammon" (Matt. 6:24). A divided heart means divided loyalties and motives.

It is interesting to observe that in Hosea 6:4 God frankly recognizes the temporary nature of any "goodness" which Israel may possess. "Your goodness is as a morning cloud." In 13:3, God indicates that because of this unstable, elusive quality of character they will perish in like manner: "Therefore they shall be as the morning cloud, and as the early dew that passeth away, as the chaff that is driven with the whirlwind out of the floor, and as the smoke out of the chimney." This reminds us strongly of Psalm 1:4–6.

4. *Worldliness* (7:8)

Holiness means separation from the things which defile. How can an unholy people maintain fellowship with a holy God? Compromise with materialism, commercialism, and idolatry of any sort will weaken and mislead God's people. Worldliness is not an outward thing, it is in the heart. Like Demas, people forsake the service of God, *"having loved this present world"* [author's italics] (2 Tim. 4:10).

Israel actually enjoyed the pleasure of sin! The people were greedy for material possessions—bread, water, wool, flax, oil, and drink (2:5). They loved their wine and doubtless became intemperate. God says that they loved "flagons of wine" (3:1), that the princes had made the king sick "with bottles of wine" (7:5). He says that they assembled themselves "for corn and wine" (7:14). Cocktail parties and social drinking are hardly modern innovations!

The people were idolatrous and worldly because they enjoyed their idol worship and felt that they profited because of it. Sin is not always a revolting, degraded-looking thing. It has an overwhelming appeal and attraction. The writer of Hebrews speaks of "the pleasures of sin" (Heb. 11:25). It is possible for people to be "lovers of pleasures more than lovers of God" (2 Tim. 3:4).

Hosea said to his generation, "Rejoice not, O Israel, . . . for thou hast gone a whoring from thy God, thou hast loved a reward upon every cornfloor" (9:1).

5. *Corruption* (9:9)

The steps led progressively downward. Rejection of the known truth, pride leading to self-sufficiency, instability and superficiality, a growing worldliness of spirit—all bore fruit in corruption of faith and practice. The entire book indicates that this corruption was both moral and spiritual.

From his earliest dealings with them, God demanded purity of his people. He called them to moral standards far above those of the nations about them. In the Mosaic law he set before them the principles which should govern their conduct. He not only wanted them to *believe* something; he wanted them to *be* something.

Moral corruption had reached staggering proportions in Israel as a result of Baalism. Hosea's own wife was a victim (3:1-3). Swearing, lying, killing, stealing, and committing adultery were common sins (4:1-2). God said that he would not punish the wives and daughters who gave way to immorality because they were encouraged to it by the inexcusable example of the men (4:13-14).

The priests no longer raised their voices in protest. They were partakers of the sins of the people. They were personally immoral (6:9). Dishonest business dealings and a growing desire to suppress and oppress others characterized them (12:7). They had sown wickedness (10:13) and it had produced a repulsive harvest. "They [the people] have deeply corrupted themselves, as in the days of Gibeah" (9:9). The reference to Gibeah applies to a horrible incident recorded in Judges 19:20. It occurred during the time when there was "no king in Israel" and conditions were chaotic. The moral conditions existing at the time were similar to those of Sodom in Lot's day (Judges 19:22-28). The abuse and death of a concubine and the subsequent action of her "husband" filled the nation with horror. They were shocked into action. In the resultant civil war, thousands of men were killed (Judges 20:8–11, 21, 25, 35).

This was one of the darkest chapters of the history of Israel and was never forgotten. Hosea likens the conditions of his day to "the days of Gibeah."

6. *Idolatry* (13:2)

In the case of Israel, idolatry was not an occasional lapse of faith; the people were committed to idolatry so firmly that Hosea felt it was almost useless to intervene (4:17). They were not play-acting. They believed in their idols. They found a strange sort of satisfaction in an image of some sort which they could actually see. They found it difficult to "walk by faith, and not by sight."

All through his book Hosea identifies idolatry with the fruits of it (4:12–14; 6:7–10). Just as worship of the true God results in holiness and stability, so worship of other gods results in corruption and confusion.

III. CENTERS OF IDOLATRY

Idol worship always constitutes backsliding on the part of God's people. It is impossible to maintain close fellowship with him and serve other gods. Evidence of serious backsliding confronted Hosea everywhere. He mentions some particularly shocking illustrations. Certain communities became noted as centers of idolatry. Hosea names several which were, at one time or another, significant in the history of Israel.

1. *Gilgal* (4:15; 9:15; 12:11)

Gilgal is identified as the first stopping place of Israel when they entered the Land of Promise (Josh. 4:19). It seems to have remained the headquarters of Israel for some little time. Samuel held court there regularly in his capacity as judge (1 Sam. 7:16). Saul was crowned there (1 Sam. 11:14–15). Various other incidents gave Gilgal a place of significance in the national life.

It was at such places, regarded almost as national shrines, that idolatry frequently flourished. There people came with sacrifices and gifts to various deities.

Amos referred to Gilgal in the same breath as Bethel. He mockingly invited the people to make their sacrifices there, but indicated that such sacrifices would be unacceptable to God (Amos 4:4–5). He warned that there was no security for the people in either place. They were not to seek supposedly sacred places but to seek God himself! (Amos 5:4–5).

2. *Beth-aven* (4:15)

Little is known of this town. The name means House of Vanity and it may be that Hosea chose it because it stands in contrast with the name Bethel (House of God). Probably, it stood close to Bethel geographically.

3. *Mizpah* (5:1)

Since several places bore this name, there is some uncertainty as to the location meant. Mizpah probably means "watch-tower," so the significance very likely lies in the fact that it commanded an outlook over a wide area. It would therefore be a favorable spot for the location of one of the many "high places."

4. *Tabor* (5:1)

No doubt Hosea refers to Mount Tabor, which is over eighteen hundred feet in height. It is a few miles west of Nazareth. This is probably the mountain referred to in Deuteronomy 33:19: "They shall call the people unto the mountain; there they shall offer sacrifices of righteousness." It may have become a place of pilgrimage and frequent sacrifice. Hosea's reference seems to indicate that it also had succumbed to the evils of idolatry and had become an accessory to evil rather than an occasion for blessing.

5. *Gibeah* (9:9)

Gibeah has already been discussed in connection with the corruption of the people. The Hebrew word means hill.

6. *Ramah* (5:8)

Here again it is interesting to note that the name is derived from a word meaning "to be high." It is mentioned in Judges 19:13, in Jeremiah 40:1, and in Isaiah 10:29. Was it also immoral and corrupt during the days of the judges? In Hosea's thinking it seems to be associated with Gibeah.

7. *Gilead* (6:8)

This Gilead may be the city mentioned in Judges 10:17–18, not far from Mizpah. Very little information is available. It is likely that Hosea's allusion to it indicates some locally known scandal or reputation for vice and crime.

8. *Samaria* (7:1; 8:5–6; 10:5, 7; 13:16)

As the capital of the Northern Kingdom, Samaria came in for scathing rebuke from several of the prophets (Isa. 7:9; Jer. 23:13; Ezek. 23:4; Hos. 8:5; Amos 8:14; Mic. 1:6). It was the influence of Jezebel which made Samaria a center of idolatry. Amos thundered against the inequities and injustices which he found there, and directed a withering blast at the wealthy, cruel society ladies of the capital city (Amos 4:1).

9. *Baal-peor* (9:10)

Peor is a mountain in the land of Moab. The combined name means "lord of Peor," and so is a name both of the place and of the Baal associated with it. This Baal was worshiped with sensual, immoral rites.

IV. GROWING A HABIT

There seems to be very little Hosea could say in defense or commendation of the people. They were almost entirely apostate and morally bankrupt. How are we to account for such complete moral and spiritual collapse?

The basis of it was a stubborn, perverse refusal to "walk in the light." God's Word makes it plain that when people sin deliberately against the truth, the results are always disastrous (4:6; cf. 1 Sam. 15:26; 2 Sam. 11:27; 12:7–12; Ezek. 2:3; Rom. 1:18, 28; 2 Thess. 2:11, 12).

BENT TO BACKSLIDING 73

God gives the truth by a patient process of revelation and instruction, "precept upon precept; line upon line" (Isa. 28:13). Whenever people prefer to follow their own sinful inclinations, they lose the truth by a similar process. "Here a little, and there a little," it slips away from them. The heart is strengthened by truth accepted and obeyed, but is weakened by truth rejected and suppressed.

Years of living in disobedience to the revealed truth will produce an increasing lack of sensitivity to it. "And they consider not in their hearts that I remember all their wickedness" (7:2). The backslider is unconscious of the fact that the marks of time and deterioration are upon him. "Strangers have devoured his strength, and he knoweth it not: yea, gray hairs are here and there upon him, yet he knoweth not" (7:9).

To such a people spiritual things seem extreme and absurd. "The prophet is a fool [in their eyes], the spiritual man is mad, for the multitude of thine iniquity, and the great hatred" (9:7).

Past blessings were forgotten or ignored. "I taught Ephraim also to go, taking them by their arms; but they knew not that I healed them" (11:3).

When backsliding becomes a habit and a fixed way of life, is there a "point of no return"? Can a nation close its eyes to the truth and go headlong down the road of defiance to the will of God, until only the certainty of judgment remains? Can individuals sin against the light so frequently that God must "give them up" to their own stubborn ways?

Paul speaks of those who are "saved so as by fire," and faced for himself the possibility of being "a castaway," that is, laid aside as unfit for further service.

Very plainly Hosea teaches that it is easy to develop habits of disobedience as well as habits of obedience. Such habits grow quickly and bear fruit abundantly in a horrible harvest of spiritual confusion and barrenness (8:7; 13:3).

FOR CLASS DISCUSSION

1. What is the difference between backsliding and what is commonly called "falling from grace?"

2. Name some further causes of backsliding in addition to those suggested in this chapter.

3. What can our churches do (1) to reduce backsliding? (2) to reclaim the backslider?

In your discussion, consider some familiar aspects of your church program and evaluate them as means of combatting the tendency of unenlisted Christians to become backsliders. For example—

Figure the total number of church members who are being utilized as workers in your Sunday school—including the class officers. How many of your church members are not even enrolled in Sunday school? Do you feel that your church has gone as far as it should in using the Sunday school to provide a place of service for every church member?

Compare the number of church members enrolled in Training Union with your total church membership. What conclusions would you draw about the need to expand this ministry as a means of combatting backsliding?

How active and persistent is your church in maintaining a visitation program for following up the individuals who are habitual absentees from Sunday school, the preaching service, Training Union, prayer meeting, and other services? To what extent does this visitation ministry give to the absentees a picture of God's incomparable love, even for his backsliding people?

---

[1] Robinson, *The Twelve Minor Prophets*, (Boston: Baker), pp. 23–25.

CHAPTER 6

I. THE BASIC REASON FOR JUDGMENT
(Hos. 11:1, 4; 12:14; 12:2; 11:9; 14:4; 1:9; 2:2; 4:1;
4:6; 7:10)

II. THE DIRECT OCCASION OF JUDGMENT

1. Open Idol Worship upon a Wide Scale (Hos. 2:5;
   4:12–13, 17; 8:4–6, 11; 10:1, 5, 8; 11:2; 13:1–2;
   14:3)
2. Vanity and Superficiality (2:13; 8:3; 9:1; 10:4)
3. The Total Lack of Humanitarian Impulses (4:1)
4. Violence, Lynchings, Riots, and Moral Depravity
   (4:2)
5. Corrupt Religious Leadership (4:6–9; 6:9)
6. Unworthy Political Leadership (4:18; 5:10; 7:3)
7. Drunkenness and Debauchery (3:1; 7:5)
8. Compromise and Worldliness (7:8; 8:9–10)
9. Deception, Lies, and Hypocrisy (10:4, 13; 12:1)
10. Dishonesty and Cruelty (12:7–8)
11. Inexcusable Self-Righteousness and Pride (12:8;
    13:6)

III. THE NATURE OF JUDGMENT

(Hos. 1:5–6, 9; 2:6, 11–12; 3:4; 4:10; 5:7, 10, 12, 14;
7:12; 8:14; 10:5–6; 11:6; 13:16)

IV. THE SEVERITY OF JUDGMENT

(Hos. 1:4, 6, 9; 2:13; 4:6, 9; 5:10, 14; 8:5; 9:7, 15;
13:7–8)

6

The Certainty of Judgment

"And they shall reap the whirlwind" (Hos. 8:7).

Amos had preached to Israel that the retributive judgment of God was sure and inescapable (Amos 1–2; 9:8–10). In the meantime, the condition of the nation had grown much worse. Amos had been sent from the hill country of Judea to announce judgment upon Israel, and having delivered his message in the spirit of Elijah, he returned to his own country (Amos 7:14–17).

Now in Israel there rose up one from among themselves to tell them with anguish of soul that judgment was inevitable. Hosea belonged to the Northern Kingdom. It was his home. They were his people. He was heartbroken over their indifference and unconcern. His ministry extended over a period of years, during which he must have pleaded with them frequently.

It ought to be noted that, through the centuries in his dealings with men, God had time and again warned them of the judgment which was imminent. He did so in the case of Noah's generation (Gen. 6:17; 2 Peter 2:5). Since Noah was a "preacher of righteousness" he must have warned his fellow men while the ark was being built.

God warned Lot and his family of impending doom for

Sodom (Gen. 19:12–14). He warned Pharaoh of his plan to bring judgment upon Egypt (Ex. 7:16–18). Through Jonah he announced that within forty days Nineveh would be destroyed (Jonah 3:4). Amos plainly declared that judgment was at hand for Israel (Amos 2:6, *et al*). Through Jeremiah, God foretold the destruction of Jerusalem and the defeat of his people (Jer. 21:3–10).

The unpopularity of the prophets was based upon the fact that they constantly preached the certainty of judgment upon unrepentant, self-sufficient sinners.

I. THE BASIC REASON FOR JUDGMENT

Amos had emphasized the truth that privilege carries with it responsibility. "You only have I known of all the families of the earth: *therefore* [author's italics] I will punish you for all your iniquities" (Amos 3:2).

Hosea came along to say that God had loved his people tenderly and faithfully. "When Israel was a child, then I loved him, and called my son out of Egypt. . . . I drew them with cords of a man, with bands of love" (11:1, 4). But they had been contemptuous of God's love. "Ephraim provoked him to anger most bitterly: therefore shall he leave his blood upon him, and his reproach shall his Lord return unto him" (12:14).

The character of God makes it impossible for him to let sin go unpunished (12:2). To close his eyes to the disobedience of his own people would defeat his purpose, namely, to make of them "an holy nation." God cannot protect and preserve a nation which bears his name and yet lives openly in apostasy and immorality.

God's wrath is not purposeless. He does not "lose his temper" and act in the sudden heat of uncontrolled fury.

People sometimes punish their children because their own patience is short. They vent their own ill temper upon the children. They resent the fact that their children dare to question or oppose the parental will. By blustering words and hasty blows they hide their own feeling of futility and inadequacy. The punishment which they mete out in such cases has no particular end in view other than to enforce their own will.

God's judgments are always disciplinary. He has a definite purpose in view. He corrects, he cleanses, he purges, he destroys in order that he may rebuild. To Jeremiah he said, "See, I have this day set thee over the nations and over the kingdoms, to root out, and to pull down, and to destroy, and to throw down, to build, and to plant" (Jer. 1:10).

God has not cast off the world and left it to its own resources. He has an eternal purpose which he is unfolding. This purpose is based upon his own perfection of character. He is "the Holy One in the midst" (Hos. 11:9).

No one book in the Bible should be made to stand by itself. Each book is a part of the revelation which God has made. To interpret rightly its message, each book must be viewed in the light of the whole. The messages of other eighth century prophets cast further light upon the basic cause for judgment. Isaiah magnifies the holiness of God (Isa. 17:7-8; 30:15; 54:5). Amos emphasizes his justice (Amos 5:24). It will be seen a little later that Hosea speaks pre-eminently of God's love (Hos. 11:1; 14:4). All of these are different facets of his divine character.

Had it not been for sin, men would have had a full and perfect revelation of God. They would have enjoyed complete and constant fellowship with him. Sin brought them to a terrible state of depravity (Gen. 6:5, 12). Even the family of Noah was sadly tainted by sin. It became necessary for God, therefore, to reveal himself to man step by step. This revelation was a gradual process, which is revealed in his Word. God led man from one truth to another. Through one prophet he emphasized a particular truth, then through another he led man still further.

In common with other great Old Testament preachers, Hosea spoke plainly of judgment upon sin, but he presented this dark picture against the background of God's amazing love. Where fear had characterized the relationship of many with Jehovah, Hosea sought to show his people that God had always dealt with them in love and that their greatest sin lay in despising such wonderful love.

Sin bears the seeds of judgment within it. It is out of harmony with God's character and is in opposition with his will. Like destructive weeds, judgment grows up and flourishes in sinful soil. Therefore, where sin abounds judgment is assured. Sin involves and results in judgment. Those who fondly imagine that they can sin without paying the penalty are sadly deceiving themselves.

Hosea's contemporaries failed to see that judgment actually accompanies sin. The two are inseparable. Their sin had separated them from God (1:9; 2:2; 4:1; 4:6; 7:10). It was destroying them already. "My people are destroyed for lack of knowledge" (4:6). "Their own doings have beset them about" (7:2). "Ephraim is a cake not turned [half-baked!]" (7:8). "Strangers have devoured his strength, and he knoweth it not: yea, gray hairs are here and there upon him, yet he knoweth not" (7:9). "Israel is swallowed up" (8:8). "Israel is an empty vine" (10:1). "O Israel, thou hast destroyed thyself" (13:9).

All of this indicates that judgment can be progressive as well as sudden and that living in sin is no less than self-destruction. Dissipation can destroy the body gradually and it usually does so. It may also lead to such extremities that it provokes to some deed of violence which results in sudden destruction. Many a suicide arrives at this tragic departure as a result of a long process of playing with sin. He feels that he has reached the "point of no return."

Hosea faced the fact that his people were following such a course, and that regardless of covenants, promises, privileges, and past blessings, there could be only one outcome unless there was a complete change in their attitude and response to God's gracious appeal.

II. THE DIRECT OCCASION OF JUDGMENT

Having seen that it is an unchanging principle that judgment accompanies sin wherever it is found and is in fact an inseparable part of sin, we may now turn to the specific reasons for judgment upon Israel.

History and experience teach us that judgment falls

upon any nation which wallows in iniquity. "Sin is a reproach to any people." In the case of Israel, however, judgment would be even more certain and severe because of her relationship to Jehovah. Hosea felt that the greatest of sins was disloyalty to God. He recoiled from idolatry with the same revulsion of feeling that decent people have toward adultery.

Idolatry was the immediate occasion for judgment. Idols, images, altars, incense, "high places," and low morals told their own story. Idolatry was bearing fruit and the harvest was ungodly living. When people serve the God who made them, he lifts them up to new spiritual heights. When they serve the gods which they have made, they sink down to the lowest levels.

Hosea's convictions were so strong and his feelings so intense that it is difficult to distinguish between passages which deal with spiritual infidelity and those which refer to actual misconduct upon the physical level. The fact is that spiritual and physical corruption and degradation were so intimately associated that it was almost impossible to disassociate them.

The picture is further confused by the fact that Baalism was a strange synthesis or blending of various ideas and customs, including worship of Jehovah. One of the dangers of modern cults lies in their ability to quote the Scriptures and to seem to support their views by misuse of biblical statements.

Hosea does not pretend to list in full all the sins of Israel, nor is it necessary for us to do so, but we ought to note some of the specific evils which marred the national life.

1. Open Idol Worship upon a Wide Scale (2:5; 4:12-13, 17; 8:4-6, 11; 10:1, 5, 8; 11:2; 13:1-2; 14:3)

What would be the reaction of a husband whose wife brazenly dressed to please other men, flirted with them, and accepted their love? What would be the reaction of a wife whose husband openly showered gifts of flowers and jewelry upon other women and shamelessly lived with them? What must be the reaction of a loving God whose people openly and almost universally bestow their affection and show their preference for idols?

2. Vanity and Superficiality (2:13; 8:3; 9:1; 10:4)

Isaiah had spoken scornfully about vain and superficial living (Isa. 3:16-23). Few things can be more repulsive and unacceptable to God than a shallow, insincere, hypocritical spirit. The heart of his message through Hosea is revealed in the words, "I desired mercy, and not sacrifice; and the knowledge of God more than burnt offerings" (6:6).

3. The Total Lack of Humanitarian Impulses (4:1)

Although each of the four great prophets of the eighth century (Isaiah, Amos, Micah, and Hosea) brings his own particular emphasis, all of them agree as to the high ethical requirements of Jehovah.

They are scathing in their denunciation of the deplorable conditions which speak of "man's inhumanity to man." Greed, cruelty, injustice, inequity, corruption, and degradation simply do not belong among a people who bear the name of the Lord.

4. *Violence, Lynchings, Riots, and Moral Depravity* (4:2)

Broken fellowship with God leads to hatred among men. Cain killed his brother. Noah's world was "filled with violence." In describing unregenerate humanity, Paul quotes the words, "Their feet are swift to shed blood" (Rom. 3:15). The atheism of France expressed itself in terrible scenes of violence during the Revolution. The godless philosophy of Nazi Germany plunged the world into a horrible blood bath.

5. *Corrupt Religious Leadership* (4:6–9; 6:9)

In common with other men, religious leaders frequently display human weakness. The fear of man, the desire for human approval, and the influence of general conditions combine to lead them into compromise and misuse of their high privileges. This danger is even more prevalent where religious life is thought of largely in terms of ritual and ceremony. The divorce of faith and practice leads, in time, to the collapse of both. Jesus spoke sharply about religious activities which are devoid of spiritual perception and depth (Matt. 23:13–33).

6. *Unworthy Political Leadership* (4:18; 5:10; 7:3)

In every realm of life, the quality of leadership is vital. Hosea's references to national leaders indicate that there was a serious lack of character at this level. He speaks of "the wickedness of Samaria," the national capital (7:1). It appears that kings, princes, and judges alike closed their eyes to existing conditions and even profited from organized corruption (5:10; 7:1–7). The reference to the removal of landmarks (5:10) refers to the land-grabbing policies of the wealthy and influential who heartlessly disinherited the poor.

7. *Drunkenness and Debauchery* (3:1; 7:5)

While Hosea does not enter into any extended discussion of the problem of alcoholic beverage, he does allude to it several times. From Noah's day to our own, it has contributed largely to the decline and decay of nations and world empires. Since alcohol removes inhibitions and inflames sensual desires, it follows that morals dip to a lower level when drinking is the order of the day.

8. *Compromise and Worldliness* (7:8; 8:9–10)

The whole book presents a picture of materialism, sensualism, and complete abandon to the pursuit of illicit and illegitimate enjoyments. Israel had become a nation of people who were "lovers of pleasure more than lovers of God." Not all of them practiced all the evils mentioned, but at least an overwhelming majority were seriously affected by the social standards about them.

9. *Deception, Lies, and Hypocrisy* (10:4, 13; 12:1)

Political intrigue and deceit was simply a symptom of national decay. Jehovah was no longer considered in the national policies of Israel. They had rejected him and turned to human diplomacy. Hosea 12:1 plainly shows that they were "playing both ends against the middle"!

10. *Dishonesty and Cruelty* (12:7–8)

There can be no doubt that the land was plagued with exorbitant taxes, hidden profits, corrupt business practices, dishonest contracts, blackmail by loan sharks, and other abominable practices. Greed makes men cruel. Hosea's indictment is that those who were in a position to do so, love to oppress and take advantage of those who are unprotected.

11. *Inexcusable Self-Righteousness and Pride* (12:8; 13:6)

A conscience seared by such practices as prevailed in Israel, ceases to function. The sense of guilt departs. In its place arises a smug complacency (12:8). Seeming success builds up a feeling of complete self-sufficiency.

Hosea's whole picture is of a rapidly deteriorating and disintegrating society, where moral and spiritual turpitude was complacently accepted or winked at. Living sinfully had become a fixed habit!

III. THE NATURE OF JUDGMENT

In Noah's day God unleashed a flood of waters. In Abraham's day he hurled fire and brimstone upon the cities of the plain. Both fire and water can be devastating and destructive. In Moses' day God used a plague of poisonous serpents. Individuals have felt the whiplash of God's wrath in various ways. They became leprous (2 Kings 5:27; 2 Chron. 26:19; Num. 12:10), they were swallowed up (Num. 16:31–33), they died violently (2 Kings 1:10, 12).

The judgment which Hosea tearfully predicted for his own nation was to fall in various ways:

1. It would involve bloody fighting. "I will break the bow of Israel in the valley of Jezreel" (1:5).

2. It would involve exile from their homeland. "I will utterly take them away" (1:6; 9:3; 9:17).

3. It would leave them completely disowned. "I will not be your God" (1:9).

4. Bewilderment and frustration would be their lot. "She shall not find her paths . . . I will also cause all her mirth to cease" (2:6, 11).

5. Drought and famine would rob the nation of material security. "I will destroy her vines and her fig trees" (2:12).

6. Leadership and support would be removed. "For the children of Israel shall abide many days without a king, and without a prince, and without a sacrifice, and without an image, and without an ephod, and without teraphim" (3:4).

7. Satisfaction and normal growth would be lost. "The floor and the winepress shall not feed them, and the new wine shall fail in her" (9:2). "For they shall eat, and not have enough" (4:10).

8. God's judgment upon them would be swift and complete (5:7), overwhelming (5:10), eating away "as a moth" and "as rottenness" (5:12), and would fall upon them with violence "as a lion . . . to tear" (5:14).

9. They would be snared and trapped like animals. "When they shall go, I will spread my net upon them; I will bring them down as the fowls of the heaven; I will chastise them . . ." (7:12).

10. Fire would eat up their cities and great buildings. "I will send a fire upon his cities" (8:14). Here is the picture of invasion, defeat, and a "scorched earth."

11. Disgrace and humiliation would be heaped upon them. "Israel shall be ashamed of his own counsel" (10: 5–6; 11:6).

12. Kings would disappear almost overnight. "Her king is cut off as the foam upon the water" (10:7). "So shall Bethel do unto you because of your great wickedness: in a morning shall the king of Israel utterly be cut off" (10:15).

13. They would be subject to foreign powers. "The Assyrian shall be his king" (11:5). Israel was to become a vassal state, a nation of slaves.

14. Terrible atrocities would horrify them. "Their infants shall be dashed in pieces" (13:16).

Why such complete and devasting judgment? Because they had violated their covenant, outraged God's love, spurned his counsel and sold themselves to sin.

IV. THE SEVERITY OF JUDGMENT

Men of every age seem to underestimate what God's Word calls "the exceeding sinfulness of sin." It follows naturally that they also underestimate the penalty of sin. The penalty matches the crime. The severity of judgment is in direct accord with the seriousness of the wrong.

Moses taught this (Deut. 28:15–20). Joshua reemphasized it (Josh. 23:6–13). Isaiah indicated that the people of his day had no appreciation of the meaning of genuine, spiritual service but were corrupt, self-satisfied, and vain (Isa. 1:2–4, 10–15; 3:16–24). Jeremiah indicated that they had lost their sense of godly fear (Jer. 5:22–24). He shows how a nation can come to the point of defiant rebellion which ignores the threat of certain judgment: "As for the word that thou hast spoken unto us in the name of the Lord, we will not hearken unto thee" (Jer. 44:16).

The writer of 2 Kings describes in detail the direct cause of the downfall of the Northern Kingdom (2 Kings 17:6–18). His description corresponds exactly with Hosea's. Note particularly verses 13–16. Sin seems to have blinded the people to the fact of God's love to them and of his hatred of sin.

Amos spoke of people who "put far away the evil day, and cause the seat of violence to come near" (Amos 6:3). In other words, they dismissed from their minds the thought of judgment, yet promoted violence and injustice, and these same people piously pretended to long for the coming of the "day of the Lord"! (Amos 5:18–20).

The judgment which Hosea predicted would be extremely severe. It would be no little pat on the wrist. God would not merely rebuke the people of Israel, but would destroy them. It is the prophet's deep conviction of the severity and finality of God's judgment which accounts for the broken, almost disconnected style of his book. Judgment was sure and was imminent but the people simply did not care! One of sin's tragedies lies in its power to destroy spiritual perception and to take away the ability to choose and act rightly.

Perhaps the most impressive way to emphasize the

severity of the judgment which was to fall upon Israel is to look at a few of God's prophetic words given through Hosea:

"I will avenge the blood of Jezreel upon the house of Jehu" (1:4).

"I will no more have mercy upon the house of Israel" (1:6).

"I will not be your God" (1:9).

"I will visit upon her the days of Baalim" (2:13).

"I will also reject thee" (4:6).

"I will punish them for their ways" (4:9).

"I will pour out my wrath upon them like water" (5:10).

"I will take away, and none shall rescue him" (5:14).

"Mine anger is kindled against them" (8:5).

"The days of recompence are come" (9:7).

"I will love them no more" (9:15).

"I will be unto them as a lion . . . as a leopard . . . as a bear . . . and there will I devour them like a lion" (13:7–8).

This list is sufficient to indicate that "the days of recompence" were going to be unbelievably severe. Idolatrous, adulterous Israel, which now enjoyed the pleasures of sin, would also suffer the full penalty for sin, which is death.

FOR CLASS DISCUSSION

1. The statement is frequently made that the God of the Old Testament is entirely different from Jesus' picture of the Heavenly Father. Does the New Testament speak of judgment? (Acts 17:30–31; Rom. 2:5–9; 2 Thess. 1:7–10; Rev.

20:11–15). What about Jesus and judgment? (Matt. 7:21–23; 11:20–24; 12:31–37).

2. Suggest some of the seeds of judgment which are already apparent in our national life.

3. What practical steps could be taken to deal with some of the major problems which threaten our national welfare?

CHAPTER 7

I. ISRAEL'S SIN DEMANDS REPENTANCE
(Hos. 2:2, 5; 4:1–2; 5:15; 10:12; 14:1–2; 2:10; 4:12; 7:1–2, 4; 9:1, 10)

II. THE CHARACTER OF GOD DEMANDS REPENTANCE
(Hos. 2:19–20; 3:5; 11:9; 12:6)

III. THE INADEQUACY OF RITUAL DEMANDS REPENTANCE
(Isa. 1:10–15; Mic. 6:6–8; Hos. 2:11, 13; 3:4; 6:9; 8:13)

IV. THE PROPHETS' PREACHING DEMANDS REPENTANCE
(Hos. 6:5; 14:1; 2:13; 4:7; 5:4, 7; 6:7; 7:13; 9:9; 10:4; 13:2)

7

The Call to Repentance

"O Israel, return unto the Lord thy God" (Hos. 14:1).

ALL the prophets were preachers of repentance. This was their divine calling. Speaking through Jeremiah, God called upon his people "to hearken to the words of my servants the prophets, whom I sent unto you, both rising up early, and sending them, but ye have not hearkened" (Jer. 26:5).

Among the favorite words of the vocabulary of the prophets were the two words "turn" and "return." They pleaded with sinful men to turn from their sin. They earnestly called upon the backslider to return to God. Repentance, as they saw it, called for decisive action. Isaiah expressed it in the words, "Cease to do evil; learn to do well" (Isa. 1:16–17). Shallow, sentimental tears would not suffice. A mere admission of guilt would not solve the problem. Outward performance of ritual would not satisfy the demands of a holy God. Something must happen in the heart which would reflect itself in the way of life. The prophets agreed with the conviction of John the Baptist, expressed much later, that people ought to "bring forth fruits worthy of repentance."

Hosea was no exception. He uses the word "repentance" only once, and that is in a rather difficult passage

(13:14) which may refer to the compassion of the Lord. However, Hosea definitely calls for repentance, again and again.

I. ISRAEL'S SIN DEMANDS REPENTANCE

Hosea's first argument for repentance is that the sin of Israel demands it. "Plead with your mother, plead" (2:2). Why? Because she had "played the harlot" (v. 5). Hers was not a minor ailment to be lightly regarded and easily treated. It was a major disease.

What was it for which Jehovah wanted to plead with the wayward nation? That she would turn from her life of sin (v. 2b). The words imply sincere, wholehearted repentance, even though they do not name it as such. Certainly she would not forsake her sinful ways until repentance came to her. The plea that God made was within itself a call to repentance.

Rightly understood, every indictment of their sin constituted a call to repentance. Hosea goes on to say that the Lord has a controversy or "lawsuit" with his people: "Hear the word of the Lord, ye children of Israel: for the Lord hath a controversy with the inhabitants of the land, because there is no truth, nor mercy, nor knowledge of God in the land. By swearing, and lying, and killing, and stealing, and committing adultery, they break out, and blood toucheth blood" (4:1–2).

In this connection, note what Micah has to say along the same line (Mic. 6:1–5). Jehovah is true but the people are untrue. He is faithful but they were unfaithful. They had plunged the whole land into violence and anarchy. Such sin demanded repentant hearts.

God expected repentance upon their part for he said, "I will go and return to my place, till they acknowledge their offence, and seek my face" (5 : 15). Confession and forsaking of sin constitute real repentance. He made it plain that they must recognize their sin, "acknowledge their offence," and then turn from it.

The next call to repentance is found in the tenth chapter in the words, "Break up your fallow ground: for it is time to seek the Lord" (10:12). The following verse indicates why: "Ye have plowed wickedness, ye have reaped iniquity." The fallow ground lay unbroken and unused and was grown up with weeds. There was need to tear out these weeds and prepare the soil to be fruitful and productive. It could be done only as there was a willingness to "seek the Lord." Repentance would pave the way for a return to him.

The most direct appeal is found in the closing chapter: "O Israel, return unto the Lord thy God; for thou hast fallen by thine iniquity. Take with you words, and turn to the Lord: say unto him, Take away all iniquity, and receive us graciously: so will we render the calves of our lips" (14:1–2).

Here is real preaching! Hosea was pleading from a broken heart and reproaching with tender yearning. People cannot be driven to repentance, but they may be loved into it. He did not hesitate to remind them of their sin, but he showed them that the door was open and that sin could be defeated if they would return with penitence and humility. All these appeals for repentance and return are seen against the dark background of national and personal corruption and unfaithfulness. Throughout the whole book the prophet is saying in effect that Israel's sin demanded repentance.

No one could possibly accuse Hosea of avoiding the issues or watering down his message. Whatever criticism he draws is more likely to stem from the very frankness of his speech. He draws a picture. It is the picture of a nation whose heart has become a moral and spiritual cesspool (2:10; 4:12; 7:1-2, 4). He did not shrink from the responsibility of placing the guilt exactly where it belongs (5:1). Sin is pictured in its true light in the preaching of Hosea. It is revealed as a loathsome, filthy, nauseating, repulsive thing (9:9-10).

Even though the prophet never used the word repentance, such preaching would constitute a clarion call to Israel to humble themselves, confess their sin, seek God's face and "turn from their wicked ways"! Fundamentally, however, it is their sin which demands repentance. Hosea's preaching simply calls attention to their desperate need of the grace of God.

II. THE CHARACTER OF GOD DEMANDS REPENTANCE

The worship of Baal did not demand repentance. An idolatrous system filled with corrupt practices contains no challenge to high moral and spiritual levels. There was nothing in the character of the Baals to lead to conviction of sin. An outward ceremonial observance of the ritual was all that was expected (2:13). Such a religion even sponsors and encourages low-level living (4:12-14).

Empty ritual is repugnant and dishonoring to the Lord (6:6; 8:13; 9:4-5; 13:2-3). The character of Jehovah is holy and righteous. To his people he says, "Be ye holy, for I am holy." His character demands something corresponding to it in the character of his people. It is impossible to worship him sincerely and live in the moral and spiritual lowlands.

Hosea's severe indictment of the people of Israel is based upon his knowledge of the character of Jehovah. Among other things Hosea recognized that God's character is marked by righteousness, justice, love, mercy, and faithfulness or integrity (2:19–20). To Jehovah the God of Israel he also ascribes "goodness" (3:5). This is from the same word used in Genesis 1:12, 18, and subsequent verses, speaking of God's creative work. He is good and what he does is good. In common with Isaiah and other great prophets, Hosea speaks of the holiness of God (11:9). By direct statement and by implication, Hosea magnifies the truth revealed so gloriously in the New Testament that "God is love."

It was because he knew God's character to be perfect that Hosea cringed at the appalling corruption all about him. He knew that God's standards were absolute and were not determined by expediency. He knew, also, that God's justice is tempered by mercy, and this knowledge gave him hope.

From his own experience Hosea knew that it was possible to forgive even the most flagrant treachery. He realized, however, that he could not fully forgive his erring wife unless she repented sincerely; neither could Jehovah forgive his people. Hosea was, therefore, preaching for repentance when he wistfully said, "Come, and let us return unto the Lord: for he hath torn, and he will heal us; he hath smitten, and he will bind us up" (6:1).

God chastises but he restores. He hurts but he heals. The prophet says in effect, "Come back to the Lord and let his chastisement bear fruit. Let us re-establish our relationship with him and then 'press on' to a more personal and intimate knowledge of the Lord."

Another appeal for repentance is found in Hosea 12:6: "Therefore turn thou to thy God: keep mercy and judgment, and wait on thy God continually." The basis for this appeal is the providential hand of God in the history of Israel ever since he appeared to Jacob at Bethel (12: 4-13).

Hosea called upon his people to remember some of the significant things which marked their relationship with God as a people. He reminded them that Jacob, even at his birth, had revealed his precocious, aggressive ways (12:3); that later in life he found the way to spiritual strength (12:4); that God spoke to him and through him; and that God had dealt faithfully with Jacob's descendants. They bore, therefore, a special relationship to God, a relationship which carried with it great responsibility upon their part.

"Therefore"—because of all this—"turn to thy God." This turning to God, or repentance upon their part, was to involve a change in their lives. They were to combine the qualities of mercy and justice in their dealings with men and were to serve God with expectancy and consistency (12:6).

Can a nation as signally blessed forget, neglect, betray, and desert the God of their fathers? Conscience, memory, and reason must combine in leading them to repentance. The character of the Lord of Hosts demands it!

III. The Inadequacy of Ritual Demands Repentance

In this connection also, Isaiah scathingly referred to the emptiness of ritual as a substitute for spiritual worship (Isa. 1:10–15). He spoke of "new moons, sabbaths, assemblies, appointed feasts." Actually, such activities on the part of God's people, when their lives are corrupt and disobedient, represent a hypocritical attitude which is revolting to the Lord.

Nothing less than a heart that is right can be acceptable to the Lord. Saul attempted to substitute a sensational sacrifice for complete obedience, and was sternly rebuked for it (1 Sam. 15:3, 8, 9, 21–22). Micah dealt with the same problem of what is acceptable to God (Mic. 6:6–8). His searching questions are followed by another which supplies the answer (v. 8b).

It is interesting that Micah uses Hosea's word *hesedh*, or mercy. It is a word which indicates a right frame of mind and heart. It expresses itself in compassion, fairness, honesty, and sincerity in our dealings with others. God requires such mercy rather than ritual and ceremony, no matter how costly or elaborate they may be. Hosea does not deal at length with this problem, but he does mention it and it is implicit in the whole picture which he presents.

The Old Testament system of sacrifices and offerings was divinely instituted. (See Ex. 29–31; 40.) The whole burnt offering, the wave offering, the peace offering, the burning of incense, the sprinkling of blood—all these were meaningful to the people of God. To evaluate the sacrifices and offerings and to appreciate the ritual and ceremony connected with them, it is necessary to stand where they stood—in the time before Calvary. In a very beautiful and pictorial manner these sacrifices prefigured the things which should later come to pass.

A priesthood was needed to minister on behalf of the people. An orderly procedure was essential, if dignity and reverence were to characterize such activities. Ritual in itself is neither evil nor repugnant to the Lord. It can express real worship and sincere service.

When ritual and ceremony were completely devoid of spiritual perception, when they were a "cover-up" for sinful practices they became an abomination to the Lord. Speaking through the lips of Hosea, God said of Israel, "I will also cause all her mirth to cease, her feast days, her new moons, and her sabbaths, and all her solemn feasts" (2:11). Two things had happened in Israel: first, ritual had become heartless and empty; second, the very services by which people once honored Jehovah had been employed in the worship of Baal (2:13).

God indicated that, because of their lapse into idol worship, he was going to take away from them the very forms, ceremonies, and religious "aids" with which they were familiar. "For the children of Israel shall abide many days without a king, and without a prince, and without a sacrifice, and without an image, and without an ephod, and without teraphim" (3:4).

The well-known words of Hosea 6:6 simply reflect again the emptiness and uselessness of a formal acquiescence to the letter of the law when the spirit is ignored. The people had been bringing burnt offerings, but their hearts were wrong. To make it worse, even the priests who ministered the sacrifices were personally corrupt (6:9). Hosea indicated that even though some of them loved to sacrifice, God had no pleasure in it; in fact, he would not accept it (8:13). Hosea seems to indicate that a day was coming when they would be deprived of even this privilege in a strange land (9:3–5).

The death of Christ upon Calvary removed once for all the necessity for blood sacrifices and the accompanying ritual. "For if the blood of bulls and of goats, and the ashes of an heifer sprinkling the unclean, sanctifieth to the purifying of the flesh: how much more shall the blood of Christ, who through the eternal Spirit offered himself without spot to God, purge your conscience from dead works to serve the living God?" (Heb. 9:13–14). The New Testament gives us the picture of a body of believers, equal in rank and privilege, meeting informally in Christ's name, without stated ritual or ceremony.

Some people find that a certain amount of ritual is helpful to them in their worship activities, but the great majority of Southern Baptists cling to an informality and freedom in worship which reduces ritual to a minimum. For us, however, there remains the same danger that our participation in the services of our churches may be impersonal and insincere.

The whole tenor of Hosea's message emphasizes the

emptiness of ritual and its total inability to meet the need of a disobedient people. Its very inadequacy is a call to repentance!

IV. THE PROPHETS' PREACHING DEMANDS REPENTANCE

Obviously, the Old Testament prophets preached for action. God intended them to do so. He said, "Therefore have I hewed them by the prophets; I have slain them by the words of my mouth" (Hos. 6:5). It was not through the ritual of the priesthood but by the preaching of the prophets that God revealed his will.

Not with worldly wisdom, not with human eloquence, not by the influence of magnetic personality, but by the power of a divinely inspired message the prophets rang the changes on the people of their day. They prefaced that message with the significant phrase, "Thus saith the Lord." God had spoken to them and his word was like a fire within their bones. They could not keep silent.

Call the roll of the prophets. They were spokesmen for Jehovah. They were witnesses to the truth at times when truth had well-nigh vanished from the earth. They were preachers of repentance. Who knows what their courageous testimony accomplished? Who can say what would have happened without it?

They were disliked, feared, persecuted. Our Lord refers to them as "my servants, the prophets." To them he revealed his plan and purpose, and they in turn told others. They were forerunners of the preachers of the New Testament.

To delete from the Old Testament the message of the prophets would be to reduce immeasurably our knowledge of the character and purposes of God. Amos said, "Surely the Lord God will do nothing, but he revealeth his secret unto his servants the prophets" (Amos 3:7).

A review of the preaching of these great, God-called men will indicate that they consistently emphasized certain great truths. They taught that Jehovah is a divine personality, "the living God" (Jer. 10:10); that he is sovereign and supreme, "the God of the whole earth" (Isa. 6:3; 54:5; 45:5–6; Amos 3:8; 4:13; Jer. 18:6–10); that he is holy (Isa. 6:3); that he is righteous and just in his dealings (Jer. 12:1; Dan. 9:14; Isa. 45:21); that he does not needlessly punish (Joel 2:12–14; Micah 7:8–9); that he values the individual (Ezek. 18:23; 33:7–16; Isa. 57:15; Hos. 14:3); that he can be approached (Nah. 1:7; Isa. 65:24); and that he will forgive sin and redeem (Isa. 1:18; Joel 2:18; Zech. 8:1–8).

All this and much more the prophets taught concerning God. Their contribution to the doctrine of God is inestimably valuable. It was Hosea's particular ministry to magnify the love of God.

Hosea must be ranked high among the prophets. He lived in difficult, troublous, impossible times. Was it too late to intervene? Had Israel passed her day of opportunity? Was he casting his pearls before swine? Sometimes he thought so. He said, "Ephraim is joined to idols: let him alone" (4:17). Such moments of despair, however, were overshadowed by an abiding conviction that God's abundant mercy could still prevail if he were given a chance.

The kind of preaching which Hosea did is always a call to repentance! He was plain-spoken without vulgarity. He was positive and personal without being vindictive. He was fearless without being belligerent. He was realistic without being totally pessimistic. He was persuasive without compromise. He was tender and compassionate without being soft and sentimental.

Put him down as a great preacher who had insight into the very heart of God because of the travail of his own heart. He felt that there was but little hope for Israel, yet he magnified that spark of hope and invited sinful men and women to renounce their stubborn ways and seek God (14:1).

Look for a moment at some of the pungent statements which demand repentance:

"And I will visit upon her the days of Baalim, wherein she burned incense to them, and she decked herself with her earrings and her jewels, and she went after her lovers, and forgat me, saith the Lord" (2:13).

"As they were increased, so they sinned against me" (4:7).

"They will not frame their doings to turn unto their God" (5:4).

"They have dealt treacherously against the Lord" (5:7).

"But they like men have transgressed the covenant: there have they dealt treacherously against me" (6:7).

"Woe unto them! for they have fled from me: destruction unto them! because they have transgressed against me: though I have redeemed them, yet they have spoken lies against me" (7:13).

"They have deeply corrupted themselves, as in the days of Gibeah" (9:9).

"They have spoken words, swearing falsely in making a covenant" (10:4).

"And now they sin more and more" (13:2).

This is the backdrop against which you read the urgent appeal, "O Israel, return unto the Lord thy God; for thou hast fallen by thine iniquity" (14:1).

We shall see as we continue the study that Hosea based his appeal upon the greatness of God's love. Israel was to come back to God because she was his wayward wife. Hosea's heart was torn with conflicting emotions as he saw her following her path that could only end in complete destruction.

Hosea spoke with a frankness which is startling, yet he did not try to beat the people into submission. Judgment must fall upon them, but the fear of judgment was not the primary basis of appeal. They belonged to God. He loved them. They had violated their sacred covenant with him. God's love was reaching out to them. Their own hearts could never be satisfied with an adulterous relationship, and God's heart was deeply grieved. "O Israel, return unto the Lord thy God."

FOR CLASS DISCUSSION

1. Look further into the meaning of repentance and the teaching of God's Word concerning it.

2. Name some of the conditions now existing which should call us to repentance as a nation; as churches; as individuals.

3. Discuss what is meant by "the goodness of God" which leads men to repentance.

CHAPTER 8

8

Discovering God's Love

"I will love them freely" (Hos. 14:4).

GOD loves and forgives. This is the heart of Hosea's message. God can be highly indignant but also deeply compassionate. His wrath can be terrible but his mercy is beyond understanding. In spite of human provocation it "endureth for ever."

God's love is always extended, for this is his very nature, but his forgiveness is conditioned upon the attitude and response of the sinner. Without repentance and return there can be no forgiveness. God can forgive and he does when the conditions of forgiveness are met.

Scholars are rather generally agreed that Hosea made a marvelous contribution to the understanding of the nature of God. His power, his justice, his wrath were widely accepted and recognized. It remained for Hosea to magnify God's love.

Brooke Peters Church says, "The idea of the love of God, a commonplace to us, but a striking innovation then, was adopted by Hosea's successors, and in time love became as much an attribute of divinity as the justice Amos preached." [1]

Hamond says, "He led the way to something that is limitless, namely, the love of God." [2]

Barnard C. Taylor says, "The love of God is used as

a background for destruction, and the destruction would be all the greater because the love was so great." [3]

John Paterson says, "To Amos love was exhausted, but to Hosea it was inexhaustible." [4]

Speaking of Hosea's own heartbreak, Dr. J. W. Storer has said, "Out of that experience, Hosea gives us a marvelously touching call to consider the deathless love of God; the exceeding sinfulness of sin; the judgment which must inevitably come to those who play him false; and then, his patient seeking and rescue of his people." [5]

T. K. Cheyne says, "Hosea was to learn what no prophet had learned before, and what no prophet ever could have learned by a mechanical revelation from without; viz. that the essence of the divine nature was not justice but love." [6]

I. GOD OF WRATH OR GOD OF LOVE?

At the moment the important thing to consider is not what is our own conviction on the vital question of wrath or love, but what was Hosea's conviction. We have the New Testament. We have the revelation of God in Christ. We have the story of Calvary. We have two thousand years of Christian history to testify to us. Hosea had none of these. What did he believe? What did he teach?

A careful study of his book will lead us to see that he teaches that Jehovah is a God of wrath because he is a God of infinite love. It is because he is capable of such matchless love that he is also capable of divine wrath. God has revealed his love, he has demonstrated his love, he has acted in love, he has shared his love. Such love outraged, rejected, and spurned, demands retribution.

Hosea uses three figures by which to emphasize the relation of Jehovah to his people: first, the relationship of father and son (11:1); second, that of husband and wife (2:16); third, that of king and subjects (13:10).

In a marked degree Hosea revealed his own love for Jehovah, for Gomer his wife, and for his own people, the nation of Israel. He learned by experience. His love for a wayward wife and a wanton, rebellious people left his heart tortured with grief.

A superficial reading of his book might give the impression that he was unnecessarily harsh. Casual readers might gather that he regarded Jehovah as a God of wrath with only occasional flashes of tenderness or compassion.

There can be no doubt that Hosea plainly taught that God punishes sin and would punish Israel for her sin. Look at some of the words which speak of punishment: avenge, break, strip, slay, hedge up, take away, discover, destroy, visit, reject, forget, punish, devour, pour out, tear, chastise, bury, recompense, bereave, drive them out, cast them away, consume, rend, anger, fierceness, wrath.

There are many, many others not included in this list. Did Hosea then picture a God of avenging wrath who delights to destroy? Did he feel that God demands the impossible and inflicts punishment upon all who cannot meet his demands? Did he picture Jehovah as a sovereign tyrant who imposes his own will without regard to the welfare of men? Did Hosea feel that the impending judgment was undeserved or too severe?

On the contrary, he recognized that God could do no less and still be true to his nature. The punishment which was about to strike was not something wilfully imposed upon the people by an angry God, but was self-inflicted (13:9). The enormity of their own sin had determined the severity of the judgment which should carry them away. They were but reaping what they had sown. God had not driven them to this extremity. He had sought to draw them from it, but they had perversely pursued their own mad course.

II. THE HEART OF GOD REVEALED

Sin separates. It separated Hosea and his wife. It separated Israel and Jehovah. It is an ugly thing. No amount of culture or refinement can make it anything else. Hosea made no effort to gloss over it. He made it just as ugly as it is.

Most of his message dealt with sin and its result. He made it plain that Jehovah would neither compromise nor temporize. Sin must be judged. However, as Hosea's heart went out to his own beloved, yet faithless, wife he realized that the heart of God yearned over his faithless people.

One of the characteristic features of the book is its swift passage from rebuke and condemnation to loving appeal. Again and again the whiplash of stern rebuke is immediately followed by a healing word of compassion. "For he hath torn, and he will heal us; he hath smitten, and he will bind us up" (6:1). Although God says with finality, "ye are not my people, and I will not be your God" (1:9), the very next verse adds, "and it shall come to pass, that in the place where it was said unto them, Ye are not my people, there it shall be said unto them, Ye are the sons of the living God" (1:10).

Having flayed the people for their heartless desertion and transfer of their affections to other gods (2:2–13), Jehovah forthwith promised to woo and win Israel back again, to open a door of hope, to renew his covenant, and to betroth her to him in "faithfulness" (2:14–23).

There is a wonderful tenderness expressed in the words of Hosea 6:1–3. Here once again the warm, gracious, forgiveness of God is magnified. A national resurrection by God's mercy is suggested in verse 2.

Who is not familiar with the words of verse 6: "For I desired mercy, and not sacrifice; and the knowledge of God more than burnt offerings." Jesus used these words as he sought to show the difference between empty formalism and real spiritual perception. Here is another glimpse into the heart of God!

Few passages are more appealing than the touching description of a father whose love for his little son is shown in his patient guidance of his tottering footsteps (11:1, 3). God says that he literally bound himself to them with strong cords of love (v. 4). His constant references to them as "my" people indicate how close and intimate had been their relationship. All of this and much more indicates that to Hosea was given unusual insight into the deathlessness of God's love.

III. MERCY IN THE MIDST OF WRATH

Someone has said that the rainbow around the throne mentioned in Revelation 4:3 may well represent "mercy in the midst of wrath." Why not? The rainbow of Noah's day was to signify that God would never again destroy the world with a flood.

The Scriptures are filled with illustrations of this great truth: the covenant with Noah (Gen. 9:12–16); God's agreement with Abraham to spare Sodom if only ten righteous were found (Gen. 18:23–33); the episode of the golden calf (Ex. 32:1–14); the provision of the serpent of brass (Num. 21:8). Calvary is the greatest illustration of all.

Amos did not have any hope for Israel, and subsequent events supported his pessimistic outlook. The judgment which he felt to be imminent and inevitable fell with finality. Hosea shared his conviction that judgment must fall. However, knowing that the wrath of God must be revealed, he found a ray of hope in God's love, which he regarded as imperishable. There are, therefore, passages in Hosea's book which shine like stars in what would otherwise appear like the unbroken darkness of a midnight sky.

One such passage is found in Hosea 2:14–23. The first portion of the chapter contains God's estimate of the revolting character of the nation's sin and a detailed description of his intended dealings with them. Their sin was sordid; his judgment must be severe.

The next verse (14) seems to be a reversal of attitude, but is actually only another illustration of the truth which we are pursuing. God's mercy shows itself in the midst of wrath. His judgment is severe but his heart is compassionate. He has no pleasure in the death of the wicked. He does not like to punish. He suffers with his people when they suffer. As the heart of a parent is pained when he chastises his children, so God's heart is tortured because of his great love.

In this beautiful passage God promises to do ten things for Israel, his wayward wife:

1. God would woo and win her again (v. 14). Temporarily at least, it seemed that the people had surrendered to the allurements of Baalism but God would not simply give them up. He purposed to restore them to faith and love. The "wilderness" may refer to the captivity of the people or the wasting of the land.

2. He would speak "to her heart" (v. 14). The words translated "speak comfortably unto her" are almost identical with the words of Isaiah 40:2, which are likewise rendered "speak ye comfortably." A literal translation would be, "speak to the heart," which is far more forceful. Here the warm, tender, personal element is emphasized.

3. God would restore the fruitfulness of her land (v. 15). The vineyards imply fruitfulness and sustenance. On several occasions Jehovah spoke of his people as being his vineyard (Hos. 9:10; Isa. 5:1, 7). They had turned to the Baals for material increase and support (2:5). He would destroy what they now enjoyed (2:12), but he would provide new vineyards in the day of reconciliation.

4. He would give her a "door of hope" (v. 15). A "door of hope"! Here is a beautiful figure of speech. Al-

though God spoke of the certainty of judgment, this did not imply that there was now nothing but hopelessness and despair.

The valley of Achor is mentioned in Joshua 7 : 16–26. Here it was that Achan sinned so grievously. God's stern judgment fell upon the people first, and then upon Achan. The latter part of verse 26 indicates that forgiveness and restoration followed. Did Hosea hold out the hope that, even in spite of Israel's present sinful condition, God would provide a place for forgiveness and restoration which should parallel the experience in the Valley of Achor?

5. God would restore her youthful songs of joy (v. 15). When Jehovah delivered his people from bondage in Egypt and destroyed Pharaoh and his army, Moses and Miriam and the people of Israel sang a song of rejoicing and praise (Ex. 15). In those early days of deliverance and experiences of fellowship with God there were frequent songs of joy.

6. God would recognize Israel as wife (v. 16). With tenderness God looked forward to the time when their close personal relationship should be restored. He longed for the time when Israel should again call him "my husband."

7. He would banish the remembrance of other gods (v. 17). We have previously noted the many names which were identified with or joined to the word "Baal." In the day of restoration every intruder must be banished. Even the memory of those false "lovers" must be erased and forgotten.

8. God would provide and protect (v. 18). Since war is dangerous and destructive, he would abolish it and give them adequate provision and real security.

9. He would "betroth" her in lovingkindness (vv. 19–20). Few passages are more tender and personal. Remember that he was talking to a faithless wife who had lived in adultery!

10. God would "have mercy upon her" (v. 23). Here the word for mercy is not *hesedh* but *ruhamah*. It is the same word used in naming Hosea's second child. It means to pity, to have mercy upon, in the sense of being compassionate. The picture is one of complete restoration.

IV. "I Will Heal . . . I Will Love"

Throughout Old Testament history up to the time of Hosea, the love of God is mentioned rather infrequently. It is often implied and frequently demonstrated but rather rarely mentioned. The duty and obligation of his people to love him is frequently emphasized.

Is not God's love to his people one of the strongest arguments against wrong living? Even more potent than the threat of punishment is the painful truth that when we sin we are hurting him. To sin against his matchless love is to be ungrateful, selfish, disloyal, and indifferent.

Who was better suited than Hosea to interpret the feelings of Jehovah or to express his message to his people? Hosea had been through a dark, lonely valley. His soul had been stretched upon the rack of tortured love. He knew what it was to see his beloved turn from him to another. He knew what it was to keep on loving in spite of faithlessness and desertion. His heart could not and would not let her go.

Through Hosea's personal experience, God was able to reveal his own indescribable love for his people. Hosea knew exactly what God meant when he said, ". . . according to the love of the Lord toward the children of Israel, who look to other gods, and love flagons of wine" (3:1).

The sixth chapter of Hosea is characterized by strong, deep emotions. The reader gets the impression that the writer's tears were perilously near the surface. An intensity of feeling lies in the words, "Come, and let us return unto the Lord" (6:1). Out of his personal knowledge of the healing, helping hand of God, Hosea reminded the people that the hand which punished them would caress them in love. They had been bruised and smitten by the hail of judgment but they would be soothed and refreshed by the gentle rain of God's blessing (6:3).

This passage brings us to the study of a significant word, which is perhaps a favorite with Hosea. It appears in 6:4 and is translated "goodness." The Hebrew word is *hesedh* and it is worth our careful consideration.

In its origin the word means desire, ardor, zeal. As related to a covenant, it implies firmness, steadfastness. It is a word which can be used equally well in speaking of God's relation to his people, of their attitude toward him, or of their relationships one with another. It implies such things as loyalty and good faith. It speaks of kindness and consideration and a heart that can be moved with compassion and forgiveness. It involves love in action upon every level of human life.

This goodness was what God was looking for among his people. "I desired mercy [*hesedh*] and not sacrifice" (6:6). He was looking for a disposition of heart and mind, not an allegiance to ritual. Since mercy, or *hesedh,* is the thing which God wants, he will deal with his people in mercy. The word is the nearest Old Testament approach we have to the New Testament words for "grace" and "love."

In the words, "O Ephraim, what shall I do unto thee? O Judah, what shall I do unto thee?" there is the same inexpressible longing in the heart of God for continued and unbroken fellowship with his people. Their faithfulness had been as short-lived as that of Hosea's wife.

God's longing to restore them is revealed again in the words, "I would have healed Israel" (7:1). He wanted to win them back, not to destroy them.

Again the yearning of his heart appears in the touching passages in chapter 11. God is looking back in retrospect to those wonderful days when by a mighty stretched out arm he delivered his people from the prison house of Egypt. By the shedding of blood, he foreshadowed the hour of redemption when he would provide eternal salvation for every prisoner of sin who would accept it.

With tender memory God looked back to those early days of the national life of his people when he led them along step by step. They had deserted him now, and unless they would repent and return only judgment remained. The very prospect of it pained his heart. It was love which prompted him to cry, "How shall I give thee up, Ephraim? how shall I deliver thee, Israel? how shall I make thee as Admah? how shall I set thee as Zeboim? *mine heart is turned within me,* [author's italics] my repentings are kindled together" (11:8).

God had "hewed" them by his prophets. He had smitten and torn them. With the plainest of speech he had scourged them, yet the book of Hosea closes with a tender appeal and gracious promise of redemption. If the prophet had previously been a whip in the hand of God to lash the conscience, he now became a gracious evangelist to win and restore. All his tender love and concern for his people finds expression in the words, "O Israel, return unto the Lord thy God" (14:1).

"Take with you words, and turn to the Lord" (v. 2). What sort of words? Repentant words; sincere words; words of confession; words of supplication and appeal; words that bespeak a changed attitude, a humble heart. God does not ask for sacrifices upon the altar. He asks for the heart. The emotions of the heart must become vocal. Confession of sin must be made (14:2); forgiveness and restoration must be entreated (14:2); thanksgiving and gratitude must be expressed (14:6).

Forgiveness is not an easy matter. It is not easy for the one who asks it; neither is it easy for the one who grants it. The only satisfactory basis for forgiveness and restoration is complete honesty and sincerity. Those who ask forgiveness must recognize their need of it.

How can anyone know that we sincerely desire forgiveness unless we express ourselves adequately? The words may be few and almost incoherent but they will reveal the condition and attitude of the heart. No one who is sullen, self-righteous, evasive, or halfhearted is in a position to ask or receive forgiveness.

Hosea's appeal was for whole-souled repentance which would show itself in a total lack of any effort by the people to justify their conduct. "Take with you words." This is the difficult part! It is never easy to say, "I have sinned, I have played the fool," but the prodigal will never get back from the far country until he makes up his mind to forget his pride and say it.

V. The God Who Restores

The prophet Joel was a great preacher of repentance. He indicated that if the people would return to God wholeheartedly, he would graciously bless them. This is wonderfully emphasized in Joel 2:25: "And I will restore to you the years that the locust hath eaten, the cankerworm, and the caterpiller, and the palmerworm, my great army which I sent among you." God's forgiveness carries with it restoration and the healing of old scars. Even where people seem to have made complete shipwreck, he can bring about transformation and restoration to a marvelous degree.

The closing paragraph in Hosea's message reflects this same conviction. Here the grace of God is magnified. He says, "I will heal their backsliding" (14:4). This would involve two things: First, it would involve forgiveness and restoration in spite of their long-continued, spiritual adultery. It would mean the renewing of a relationship broken by sin. The repentant wife would turn from her lovers and come back to her husband. Second, it would involve deliverance from the backsliding habit. All would be in vain if she should simply return again to her adulterous ways. Her heart must be changed and she must renounce her false gods forever (14:3).

In the light of the strong condemnation of the people's sin, only a God of grace could hold open such a hope. Hosea 2:14–23 should be carefully studied in connection with 14:4–9. Note particularly the language of 2:19, "in lovingkindness, and in mercies."

In spite of the terrible sin of the people with all of its implications, Hosea believed that God's love would triumph and that a day of happy reconciliation would arrive. The prophet draws a wonderful picture of comfort, hope, affection, and continuing loyalty (2:14–16, 19–20). "And I will have mercy upon her that had not obtained mercy; and I will say to them which were not my people, Thou art my people; and they shall say, Thou art my God" (2:23).

The fourteenth and final chapter of the book closes upon a similar note. Hosea pictures their spiritual drought as being replaced by the refreshing dew which causes abundant growth and fruitfulness (14:4–7). Idolatry had led them astray, deceived them, well-nigh destroyed them, but their eyes would be opened, and in that day Israel would say, "What have I to do any more with idols?" (14:8). It would be a sad lesson learned by bitter experience in which both Jehovah and his people had suffered greatly. The present picture was dark but there was still "a door of hope." It was the greatness of God's love.

FOR CLASS DISCUSSION

1. Give a definition of love.

2. Try to recall several Old Testament illustrations of God's love.

3. Discuss God's love and his wrath with a view to harmonizing the two. In what ways can his wrath be turned aside? How does his love become effective in our case?

[1] Brooke Peters Church, *The Private Lives of the Prophets,* (New York: Rinehart, 1953), p. 89.

[2] Hamond, *The Eighth Century Prophets,* (out of print).

[3] Taylor, *Prophecy and the Prophets,* (out of print).

[4] John Paterson, *The Goodly Fellowship of the Prophets,* (New York: Scribner, 1948), p. 42.

[5] J. W. Storer, *The Major Messages of the Minor Prophets,* (Nashville: Broadman, 1940), p. 23.

[6] T. K. Cheyne, *The Cambridge Bible—Hosea,* (New York: Cambridge University Press, 1899), p. 21.

CHAPTER 9

I. NATIONAL WEAKNESS AND STRENGTH
(Hos. 1:2, 4, 6; 3:4; 5:1, 5; 7:2, 5, 7; 8:4, 10; 12:1; 13:10-12; 14:7)

II. IMPORTANCE OF HOME LIFE
(Hos. 2:10, 12; 3:2-3; 4:2, 13; 5:7; 9:9; Matt. 19:8)

III. DANGERS IN COMPROMISE
(Hos. 4:4, 8-9, 14; 4:6; 11:7; 13:2; 5:13; 7:3-7, 8-9, 11; 8:9-10; 10:4; 12:1)

IV. RIGHTLY UNDERSTANDING GOD'S LOVE
(Hos. 2:13; 4:6b; 6:4; 11:8; 2:14-23; 14:1-8; 11:9; 7:16; 11:1, 3-4; 14:1-4)

V. THE HANDWRITING ON THE WALL
(Amos 3:8; 9:8)

VI. "WHO IS WISE?"
(Hos. 14:9; 2:1, 16; 4:12; 9:1; 8:7; 10:13; 4:1-6; 14:1-2, 4; 9:1-7; 6:6; 2:15-19; 6:4; 11:8; 14:4-8)

9

Hosea's Message for Today

"It is time to seek the Lord" (Hos. 10:12).

IN some circles there is a feeling that the Old Testament is obsolete and relatively valueless. Some years ago in conversation with her pastor, a young Baptist woman in another state observed, "Of course, everyone knows the Old Testament is N.G. today." Her pastor said, "Just what do you mean by N.G.?" She replied, "Why, I mean it's 'no good' to us."

She was reflecting the thinking of a good many people who have been led to believe that the Old Testament has no value in our day. They assume that the New Testament has entirely superseded the Old and that it is a waste of time and, in fact, a mistake to consult the Old Testament in spiritual matters.

Jesus said, "Search the Scriptures." He was referring to the Old Testament. He quoted from the Old Testament constantly. He said that he came not to destroy but to fulfil the law. He began with Moses and the prophets and "expounded unto them *in all the scriptures* [author's italics] the things concerning himself" (Luke 24:27).

In the New Testament, God has revealed himself more fully. In Christ he has given us the greatest revelation of his love and purpose, but he has also revealed himself

123

in the Old Testament Scriptures. The Old Testament is divinely inspired. It is just as much the Word of God as the New Testament.

The messages of the prophets are ageless and timeless. Frequently, they deal with great principles and truths which apply to every age. It was not through the priesthood with its ritual and ceremony that God revealed himself, but through "his servants the prophets." The authoritative note in their messages rests in the oft-repeated phrase, "thus saith the Lord." They did not speak *of* themselves or *for* themselves. They were spokesmen for God.

The prophetic commission and authority is illustrated in the case of Ezekiel, to whom God said: "Son of man, I send thee to the children of Israel . . . for they are impudent children and stiffhearted. I do send thee unto them; and thou shalt say unto them, Thus saith the Lord God. And they, whether they will hear, or whether they will forbear, (for they are a rebellious house,) yet shall know that there hath been a prophet among them" (Ezek. 2:3-5).

Hosea stands tall among the prophets. He had a message for his own day and delivered it faithfully among an "impudent and stiffhearted" people. He has a message for our day. Who can read his book without being conscious of the fact that "there hath been a prophet among them"?

A brief summary of a few pertinent truths emphasized by Hosea will indicate how appropriate and timely is his message for today.

I. NATIONAL WEAKNESS AND STRENGTH

Through the years national boundaries had been exceedingly fluid and unstable. The fortunes of the nations ebbed and flowed like the tides. Sometimes they enlarged (at the expense of their neighbors), sometimes they shrank when the tide turned against them. World empires rose and fell and, in the course of their conquests, smaller nations were frequently swallowed up. It was a miracle of divine providence that Israel and Judah survived as long as they did, for they were small nations at the best.

During at least the earlier part of Hosea's ministry Israel seems to have felt no particular pressure from Syria. Assyria was not particularly aggressive until after the ascension of Tiglath-pileser (Pul). This period of comparative quiet may have accounted for Israel's complacency.

Hosea was far from complacent. He saw the nation's impending doom and sought desperately to save it. Hosea thought and spoke in terms of national sin and national judgment (1:2, 4, 6; 3:4; 5:1, 5; 7:2, 5, 7 [rulers]; 8:4, 10; 12:1; 13:10–12). He was much more concerned about inner decay than about the threat of outward violence. Israel's own moral and spiritual decline were regarded by him as far more serious than any threat of attack from without. He believed that God would be a wall of protection to his people if they would but walk with him. Hosea pictured a period of security and peace after they returned to God (2:18; 3:5; 14:7).

Hosea's message reminds every modern nation that spiritual decay, pride, drunkenness, immorality, and gross materialism pave the way to national judgment and defeat.

It is a matter of encouragement that President Eisenhower offered prayer at his inauguration, that senators and congressmen meet frequently for "prayer breakfasts" in our national capital, and that at his inauguration in recent days the governor of one of our states substituted a spiritual session for the usual cocktail breakfast.

Hosea saw no hope of national stability and security apart from dependence upon God. "O Israel, thou hast destroyed thyself; but in me is thine help. I will be thy king: where is any other that may save thee in all thy cities? and thy judges of whom thou saidst, Give me a king and princes?" (13:9-10).

II. IMPORTANCE OF HOME LIFE

Hosea's own love story and tragic home life, revealed only partially in the brief, almost incoherent narrative in chapters 1 and 3, lend much weight to this important theme. His words to his sinning wife at the time of her redemption and return speak of his own high standards for home life (3:2-3). His own broken home life says eloquently to all of us that it can happen to anyone.

His references to lewdness (2:10), lovers (2:12), the harlot (3:3), committing adultery (4:2), daughters and brides committing adultery (4:13), begetting "strange children" (5:7), moral corruption (9:9), and general low standards cry out against each outrage of decency.

Hosea's message needs to be evaluated in the light of present trends and conditions. Anyone who is complacent about the home life of America today is either blind or indifferent!

In some areas of our country three out of every five marriages end in the divorce court. In many other cases where marriages technically hold out there is constant infidelity and lack of conscience over broken vows.

Ours is a complex economic age, in which increasing participation by women in business and professional responsibilities leaves less and less time for homemaking. Relatives, friends, baby sitters, and maids serve as substitutes for mothers in the homes. Family participation in home activities becomes negligible. Lack of planned common interests leaves a vacuum from which teenagers seek to escape, and so fall an easy prey to delinquency. Is the biggest problem "adult" or "juvenile" delinquency?

Our age is caught up in the baleful influence of a "sex cult" sponsored largely by Hollywood. The glorification of the female body, of marital infidelity, of adventures in the realm of sex, all tend to destroy ideals and standards and weaken moral stamina.

Hosea's undying love for his faithless wife and his willingness to restore and forgive her is a rebuke to the hardhearted, unforgiving spirit of our age which finds divorce easier than reconciliation. Those who contemplate divorce ought to hear again the voice of Jesus saying, "Moses *because of the hardness of your hearts* [author's italics] suffered you to put away your wives: but from the beginning it was not so" (Matt. 19:8).

In the thinking of Hosea, moral and spiritual defection were inextricably bound together. The basis of true marriage is spiritual, not merely physical. Could it be that Hosea's example and deep conviction concerning personal standards and conduct are now calling pastors, churches, and people to a re-evaluation of our complacent, easygoing approach to a major problem?

III. DANGERS IN COMPROMISE

Hosea makes it plain that there was compromise on the part of the spiritual leaders (4:4, 8–9). The priests seem to have adjusted their consciences to the standards of the people. Again and again the Bible emphasizes the importance of strong spiritual leadership. The pages of history testify to the rapid decline and disintegration of a people whose religious leaders are corrupt.

Although it does not appear on the surface in Hosea's message, it is to be remembered that there had been an integration of Jehovah worship and Baalism. This involved a definite compromise of conviction and a corresponding lowering of standards. One illustration of the outcome of such compromise is to be found in 4:14. The rendering, "For the men themselves go aside with harlots and sacrifice with cult prostitutes," is probably fairly accurate.

Any compromise on the spiritual level will result in broken fellowship (4:6), drifting (11:7), and increasing disobedience (13:2). New Testament churches are challenged to avoid any sort of surrender to compromise (Acts 5:29; Rom. 12:2, 9; 14:19; 1 Cor. 10:21; 2 Cor. 6:14–17; Eph. 5:11–13).

Hosea dealt considerably with the pitfalls of political intrigue and expediency. He held firmly to the fact that Israel was a covenant people and under obligation to seek and to follow the leadership of Jehovah. He accused the nation of seeking help from Assyria when in desperate circumstances (5:13). He implied that there was a great deal of internal, undercover intrigue and trickery (7:3–7). He referred to Israel's habit of making compromising contacts and alliances with "strangers" (7:8–9). They could not decide whether to woo the favor of Assyria or Egypt, or both (7:11). The same policy of appeasement is mentioned in 8:9–10. The hypocrisy and deceitfulness of their political relationships is reflected in 10:4. This policy led them deeper and deeper into a "refuge of lies" (12:1).

It is hardly necessary to remind ourselves that the nations of our modern world are engaging in the same sort of intrigue and political jockeying. Policies are dictated by economic interests rather than by principles of justice and truth.

Sir Winston Churchill said during World War II that the people of England had determined that they "would rather die as free men than to live as slaves." It would be better for any nation to die in the cause of righteousness and justice than to prosper in the paths of deceit and dishonesty.

IV. RIGHTLY UNDERSTANDING GOD'S LOVE

Hosea's great contribution to our Christian faith lies in his grasp of the wonderful truth of God's love. No other prophet of the Old Testament had a clearer understanding or greater appreciation of the matchless, forgiving love of God. It became clear to Hosea that God suffers, and suffers deeply, when his people fall into sin.

God grieves because they have forsaken and forgotten him. He is grieved by the knowledge that he must punish them (2:13; 4:6b; 6:4; 11:8). We are to remember that Hosea spoke for God. The message came to him by revelation. He was saying to Israel the things God wanted him to say. The strong language, the deep undercurrent of feeling came not alone from Hosea's heart but from the heart of God.

Divine indignation against inexcusable conduct flames at times like a fire, but it is tempered by infinite love and compassion. Hosea presents a true picture of God's love. Not for a moment would he agree with the modern conception of God as a benign, benevolent "Grandfather" swayed by a mere sentimentalism. Hosea believed that God loves and forgives but his forgiveness is conditioned upon the sincere repentance of his people. Apart from repentance and return he saw no hope.

The two outstanding passages in his book which reveal the tenderness of God's love are 2:14-23 and 14:1-8. The fourteenth chapter particularly reminds us of the return of the prodigal and the father's compassionate love, as revealed in Luke 15:11-24.

Hosea's conception of salvation, therefore, rested upon his conception of the nature and character of Jehovah. He believed and taught that God is holy (11:9), that he is sovereign (7:16), that he has no desire for vengeance (11:9), that he has a personal relationship to his people and a personal affection for them (11:1, 3-4), and that he does forgive when sin is confessed and forsaken (14:1-4).

The superficial, popular approach to spiritual things in our day rests upon a sentimental basis and disregards the need for repentance and renunciation of sin. Hosea's message would remind us that there is no way back to God other than the recognition of our desperate need of his forgiving grace.

In the preaching of Hosea is a foregleam of Calvary. Dr. Clovis Chappell in his book *And the Prophets* says that the cross is not a single episode in the life of God. It is what he is suffering from everlasting to everlasting for the sins of his people.[1]

Hosea is saying in effect what John said later in so many words, that God is love. This is the very essence of his divine nature. Only a divine, inexhaustible, immeasurable, redemptive love could possibly say: "I will betroth thee unto me for ever; yea, I will betroth thee unto me in righteousness, and in judgment, and in lovingkindness, and in mercies. I will even betroth thee unto me in faithfulness: and thou shalt know the Lord" (2: 19-20). Only such a love could hold open a door of hope to those who had plumbed the depths of degradation and iniquity and could say, "I will heal their backsliding, I will love them freely" (14:4).

Here is the spirit of evangelism! If national affairs were at a low ebb in Hosea's day and if world conditions were confused, it is even so today. God's wrath and God's love met at Calvary—his wrath against everything that is evil but his love for the individual. It is the "goodness" of God that now calls men to repentance.

V. THE HANDWRITING ON THE WALL

Belshazzar saw the handwriting on the wall. It filled him with fear and foreboding. His fears were well-founded. For him the "days of recompense" were come!

Amos saw the handwriting on the wall. He read it rightly. He said, "The lion hath roared, who will not fear?" (Amos 3:8). Speaking of Israel he continued, "Behold, the eyes of the Lord God are upon the sinful kingdom, and I will destroy it from off the face of the earth" (Amos 9:8).

Hosea saw the handwriting on the wall. It spoke of judgment swift and sure, deadly and devastating. In a previous chapter we have considered the certainty of judgment. There was one hope, and one hope only. That hope was repentance upon a national scale. Such repentance was never realized, and judgment fell.

The Old Testament historians testify that both Israel and Judah forsook God and, though he pleaded with them to the last moment, a strange, perverse, obstinate spirit prevailed—their own sins destroyed them. They preferred their sin to God's grace.

A complacency rests upon us as a nation which should give us considerable concern. In spite of certain evidences of a renewed interest in "religion" there remain many disturbing factors. Church membership is at an all-time high, but so is the total population. Careful inquiry reveals the fact that in many cases church membership does not necessarily mean too much. Does it call for repentance? personal faith? a new birth? a change in character and conduct? conviction? ideals? standards? loyalty to Christ and his kingdom?

What of the present tendency to popularize Christianity? to glamorize it? to present it as a means of relief from tension and worry? to pattern its songs after the sentimental songs of the day?

What of the fact that sin is refined and made respectable? The lovely cocktail lounge replaces the dirty saloon; the "man of distinction" adorns the liquor advertisement; the lovely, gracious hostess always keeps the right brand of beer on hand; attractive young women extol the excellencies of their favorite brand of cigarettes; drunkards are merely "alcoholics"; divorce and remarriage are to be regretted, but are no longer considered to involve any real transgression of God's law.

The average church member can do anything he pleases and still be "in good standing." Church discipline has been almost relegated to the Dark Ages! To the man on the outside who is personally acquainted with scores of church members, what does church membership really mean?

The nation spends approximately ten billion dollars annually on alcoholic beverages. Other billions go for gambling, organized vice and crime, and a flood of printed matter unworthy of the name literature. Only some three billion dollars per year are given for religious and welfare purposes.

Sunday has become a day for intensified business activity in scores of areas and a field day for commercialized sports and private pleasures.

Our resources, our wealth, our military might, our claim to democratic ideals and practices become our boast. Like Israel of old, we assume that God is on our side and that he is bound to protect us and prosper our cause.

Compare Hosea's day with our own. Replace the altars of Baal with the modern idols of materialism, sensualism, secularism, and religious liberalism and compromise. Is there a call to repentance? How long can any nation survive when the foundations are undermined by godless living? If atomic warfare engulf us, could it be the judgment of a righteous God who has plainly told us that privilege involves responsibility?

VI. "Who Is Wise?"

"Who is wise, and he shall understand these things? prudent, and he shall know them? for the ways of the Lord are right, and the just shall walk in them: but the transgressors shall fall therein" (Hos. 14:9). Unquestionably, Hosea belonged to that noble succession of divinely called preachers to whom God refers as "my servants the prophets." His message does not flow evenly and smoothly but bursts out in explosive spasms of grief, anger, and compassion. Although he follows no carefully conceived, orderly arrangement, his preaching, nevertheless, emphasizes certain great truths which stand out clearly:

1. God's people bear a personal relation to him which is best illustrated by the marriage bond—intimate, sacred, permanent (2:1, 16).

2. Idolatry of any sort means the transfer of affection from God to some other object or person, and constitutes spiritual adultery—the breaking of a sacred bond (4:12; 9:1).

3. Sin carries the seeds of judgment within it and always bears fruit. No one can play with it with impunity (8:7; 10:13).

4. God punishes sin—especially sin in the hearts of his own people. The high privileges which he has bestowed upon them demand a corresponding sense of responsibility on their part (4:1–6).

5. There is no easy road to forgiveness and restoration (14:1–2).

6. Only sincere and wholehearted repentance can pave the way to a renewed fellowship (14:1, 4).

7. National apostasy and idolatry will inevitably mean national disintegration and destruction (9:1–7).

8. God can never be satisfied with superficial, formal, external ritual (6:6).

9. God's heart is filled with a tender, gracious, inexhaustible love (2:15, 19–20; 6:4; 11:8; 14:4–8).

10. The Old Testament as well as the New clearly teaches that "God is not willing that any should perish but that all should come to repentance."

Is our age wise enough, prudent enough to hear and heed Hosea's message?

FOR CLASS DISCUSSION

1. Suggest some of our own points of national strength or weakness. List them side by side.

2. Discuss practical means of strengthening home ties.

What about premarital counseling? seminars for young married couples? stronger ties with the church?

3. List some of the activities regarded as "worldly" and seek to evaluate their influence upon spiritual life and testimony.

4. Talk about evangelism, revival, and personal witnessing in the light of Hosea's message.

[1] Clovis Chappell, *And the Prophets*, (Nashville: Abingdon Press, 1946), p. 83.

QUESTIONS FOR REVIEW AND EXAMINATION

CHAPTER 1

1. In what century did Hosea preach?
2. Did he preach in Israel or Judah?
3. Name some of the conditions which existed in Israel at that time.
4. How does God reveal his truth to the hearts of his messengers?

CHAPTER 2

5. Do you believe that God would ask his prophet to marry an evil woman? If not, state your reason.
6. Why was Hosea's third child named Lo-ammi?
7. How did Hosea go about redeeming his erring wife?
8. What parallel do you find between Hosea's home life and Israel's relation to God at that time?

CHAPTER 3

9. What does it mean to commit spiritual adultery?
10. What leads a people to lose their sense of values?
11. Suggest some of the fruits of idolatry.
12. Discuss briefly some ways in which present-day Christians compromise.

CHAPTER 4

13. Why does the Lord use marriage as an illustration of his relation to his people?
14. Suggest three or four things which characterize marriage.
15. Name some of the results of Israel's unfaithfulness to God.
16. How can people be restored to their "first love"?

CHAPTER 5

17. How can you know when people are backslidden?
18. What caused Israel to backslide?
19. Name three centers of idolatry in Israel.
20. What happens when people sin against the truth deliberately?

CHAPTER 6

21. What was the basic reason for God's judgment upon Israel.
22. Suggest a few of the things which Hosea named as demanding judgment from God.
23. What sort of judgment did God promise?
24. How severe is God's judgment upon unconfessed and unforgiven sin?

CHAPTER 7

25. Name some of the things which demanded repentance on the part of Israel.
26. Give a definition of repentance.
27. Is there value in ritual? If so, what?
28. Discuss Hosea as a preacher.

CHAPTER 8

29. Is judgment self-inflicted? How?
30. Suggest two or three passages in Hosea which reflect the greatness of God's love.
31. What did Hosea mean by "a door of hope"?
32. Did Hosea feel there was any hope for sinning Israel?

CHAPTER 9

33. Why do we regard the Old Testament as valuable for our day?
34. Name several evidences of weakness in the Israel of Hosea's day.
35. Illustrate God's mercy and also his wrath.
36. Suggest several of the great truths emphasized by Hosea.
37. In your judgment what is the keynote of his message?

DIRECTIONS FOR THE TEACHING AND STUDY OF THIS BOOK FOR CREDIT

I. DIRECTIONS FOR THE TEACHER

1. Ten class periods of forty-five minutes each, or the equivalent, are required for the completion of a book for credit.
2. The teacher should request an award for this book.
3. The teacher shall give a written examination covering the subject matter in the textbook. The examination may take the form of assigned work to be done between the class sessions, in the class sessions, or as a final examination.

EXCEPTION: All who attend all of the class sessions; who read the book through by the close of the course; and who, in the judgment of the teacher, do the classwork satisfactorily may be exempted from taking the examination.

4. Either Sunday school or Training Union credit (to *Young People and Adults only in Training Union*) may be had for the study of this book. Application for Sunday school awards should be sent to the state Sunday school department, for Training Union awards to the state Training Union department, where forms may be secured on which to make application. These forms should be made in triplicate. Keep the last copy for the church file, and send the other two copies.

II. DIRECTIONS FOR THE STUDENT *

1. *In Classwork*

(1) The student must attend at least six of the ten forty-

* NOTE: *The student must be fifteen years of age or older to receive Sunday school credit. Training Union credit on this book is not granted to Juniors and Intermediates.*

five minute class periods to be entitled to take the class examination.

(2) The student must certify that the textbook has been read. (In rare cases where students may find it impracticable to read the book before the completion of the classwork, the teacher may accept a promise to read the book carefully within the next two weeks. This applies only to students who do the written work.)

(3) The student must take a written examination, making a minimum grade of 70 per cent, or qualify according to *Exception* noted above.

2. *In Individual Study by Correspondence*

Those who for any reason wish to study the book without the guidance of a teacher will use one of the following methods:

(1) Write answers to the questions printed in the book, or

(2) Write a summary of each chapter or a development of the chapter outlines.

In either case the student must read the book through.

Students may find profit in studying the text together, but where awards are requested, individual papers are required. Carbon copies or duplicates in any form cannot be accepted.

All written work done by such students on books for Sunday school credit should be sent to the state Sunday school secretary. All of such work done on books for Training Union credit should be sent to the state Training Union secretary.

III. THIS BOOK GIVES CREDIT IN SECTION I OF THE SUNDAY SCHOOL TRAINING COURSE.